- LDS STORYMAKERS -

Publishing SECRETS

- LDS STORYMAKERS -

Publishing Secrets

A Comprehensive Guide to Getting Your Book Published in the LDS Market

LDStorymakers, Inc.

The individual views and opinions expressed herein are the sole responsibility of their respective authors and/or contributors, and are not to be construed or interpreted as authoritative, contractual, or binding in any way.

LDS Storymakers: Publishing Secrets

Published by LDStorymakers, Inc.
P.O. Box 468, Orem, Utah 84059-0468

Cover images used with permission

ISBN 0-9749241-0-5

Printed in the United States of America
Year of first printing: 2004

10 9 8 7 6 5 4 3 2 1

Dedicated to Storymakers everywhere.

TABLE OF CONTENTS

introduction

by Gordon Ryan

So you want to be a writer?

That puts you in league with millions of other people in the world who feel, or know, that they have a story somewhere deep down in their soul. And, truth be known, they probably do.

To be clear from the start, this is primarily a book about how to get *published* in the LDS market. It is not our intention to publish a book about how to write. There are hundreds of those already available, although you will find that some of the advice presented here deals directly with writing. It's impossible to actually separate the two. But our intent is to help you learn some of the pitfalls, along with the success stories, as they apply to finding a publisher after you have done the necessary writing.

Although I have worked all of my professional career in city management, true creative satisfaction did not come until I decided I was going to write a novel. And that decision—for those of you who think life has passed you by—did not happen until I was nearly fifty. I have since published eight novels. However—and this is a very important point—*I did not give up my day job.* Thousands of successfully-published writers maintain full-time employment—including the majority of the authors represented in this book—because they have a mortgage, and they have grown fond of eating. It is a gross misconception to think that someone who publishes a book reaps instant financial rewards, including a condo in Hawaii! This is even more true with regards to the relatively small LDS literary market.

The authors in this book (and notice I did not say *writers*, I said *authors*) range from their mid-twenties to those who are in their sixties (*early* sixties, please). Some wanted to write since they crawled up to their mother's typewriter. Some, like myself, while reading a particular book, decided very late in their lives that *"I could write as well as this guy."*

Since I became associated with *LDStorymakers*—a worldwide, online group of published authors, originated by best-selling author Rachel Ann Nunes—I have been pleasantly surprised to learn of the diversity of reasons, and in some cases obsessions, that brought us all to write.

You bought this book for a reason.

We can assume that you have at least a modicum of interest in writing. As you peruse the contents of this book, we sincerely hope it will heighten your interest, spur your desire, and fulfill your need to know about the business.

Business, I say? Yes, for writing is just that—a business. It's not merely an artistic effort or something that we do on a whim or when the mood strikes. If you truly want to be an author, not just a writer, you need to write nearly every day, whether it's good or bad. Some days I write lousy scenes, other days it flows perfectly. But I write. Daily. Except Sundays or when I want a weekend off. I also usually take a few weeks break when I finish one novel before starting the next. And when I'm on holiday, I have been found on the beaches of Mexico, Hawaii, and Australia with a draft manuscript and a red pen in hand. It's a very compelling business.

If I learned anything those first few weeks and months when I sat down to show Tom Clancy that he was about to have some competition, it was that professional writing is like any other worthy endeavor. It is an exercise in discipline. A publisher won't accept the many and varied excuses: "my kids are sick, my spouse needed the computer, I couldn't think of anything," etc. And they won't accept poor spelling, terrible grammar, and shoddy manuscripts, just because "the story is so compelling." Those days, if they ever existed, are gone.

Many of these *LDS Storymakers* are mothers, with three, four, five, six, or more children—or fathers with full-time jobs and other miscellaneous responsibilities. They have no more time each day than you do. Probably less discretionary time. But, year after year, they turn out a novel. Rachel Ann Nunes, with six children, has her twentieth novel in pre-production. I imagine some days she feels like it's *six* novels and *twenty* children, but she writes, every workday. That is the kind of dedication it takes to become a published author.

The personal rewards, however, are great.

The very first time I saw my book displayed in Deseret Book's window in Zion's Mall, I had a feeling like I'd never had before. I had three children and two grandchildren by then, but *my new baby had been born*!

Such joy awaits you, too!

The folks in this book will sit in your lounge with you, kick off their shoes, lean back comfortably in *your* recliner, and carry on a conversation. The format is just that—a conversation about publishing. Listen closely. These folks have "been there, done that." I admire them all. I honor them all. They have fulfilled their dreams and are continuing to pursue their future aspirations as well. And more than that, they have entertained thousands of people, all the while teaching high moral values and eternal principles. As LDS *"every-member-a-missionary"* people, what more could we ask?

I know that the authors in *LDS Storymakers: Publishing Secrets* all have that same overriding goal: To uplift and encourage their readers. So delve in, read what they have to say, then get in front of the keyboard. And don't forget to buy a few reams of paper so you can print out and proof-read the next Great LDS Novel. You, too, will sit in awe as *your* new "baby" is prominently displayed in bookstores across the nation.

It could happen, you know! It really could.

Gordon W. Ryan
Christchurch, New Zealand

chapter 1 Honey, Take Out the Garbage

The Selective LDS Audience

by Tristi Pinkston

with contributions by
Julie Wright & Rachel Ann Nunes

So you decided to become a writer for the LDS market.

Good for you!

There are few things more rewarding than a job that allows you to share pieces of who you are and what you believe. You will discover a sense of satisfaction as you put your thoughts and feelings into words to present to others.

The LDS market can be tricky, however.

The scriptures tell us to read from the best books, and our leaders tell us to make sure that the literature in our homes is uplifting. It can be difficult to find nationally-published books that follow those guidelines, and that's why the LDS market is booming.

Let's take a look at some of the various genres and categories in the field and find out what is most likely to be successful with the LDS audience and what is generally not acceptable.

SUSPENSE/ACTION

Let's start with the popular action-adventure novel.

The main concern with writing books of this genre is the violence that generally accompanies it. Violence is a fact of life. But graphic descriptions of violence do not attract LDS readers.

Gunplay should only be used when needed. Hunting game would be an obvious exception. But when people are shooting at each other, use care in not using vivid wound descriptions.

[Rachel] I remember one particular scene in my adventure romance novel Love on the Run *where there is a huge shoot-out between the bad guys and the good guys in a remote cabin. Though the main characters get away, a few of their companions don't make it, and more than a few of the bad guys are killed. But there's no mention of blood. Plenty of falling over and lying still, but no mention of blood until much later when the FBI agent comes on the now-quiet scene. Even then it's not graphic.*

Does the lack of blood lessen the impact?

Perhaps for some, but I think LDS readers generally will appreciate your reserve, and a skilled writer can transmit the feeling of mayhem without being graphic.

This is also true with violence.

They will fill in the gaps within the realm of their personal experience. For example, a younger reader will imagine the scene much differently than an adult. Our job as the writer—and it's an obtainable goal—is to create scenes that appeal to a wide range of LDS readers.

Keep in mind that no matter whom we intend our audience to be (i.e. adults), many of our readers are very young, and their LDS mothers who buy the books are more concerned about violence than is the world at large.

Use your writing skill to create tension; it drives up sales far more than those vivid descriptions of blood and horror.

MYSTERY

[Tristi] Millions of murder mystery novels are available for sale every day. We all enjoy the challenge of trying to figure out whodunit before they strike again. But murder can be messy—and that's where caution comes into play with an LDS novel.

The human body contains a lot of blood. This is not a bad thing while we're alive; in fact, it's very useful. But once a body is dead—especially if it was murdered—it may just come out, sometimes all over the place. And that is not good in the LDS market. Gory descriptions of blood and guts are not found here. Generally speaking, if a murder takes place in an LDS novel, it's alluded to in vague terms and hints.

Why? Again it comes down to the offense factor. There is no way to safely judge how much blood ought to be allowed in the book, so it's best to take the high road and stick with hints. Many readers "gross out" easily, and you want to keep their business. Do what you can to stay within the realm of acceptability.

[Julie] A murder mystery written with artistic skill doesn't need to succumb to the shock factor of blood and guts. A writer can focus on the mystery . . . the unseen rather than the seen. If you work it right, you can end up with a mystery that twists and turns and surprises the reader at the end with someone they never would have suspected. Using blood and guts to hold a reader's attention is kind of like action thriller movies that focus entirely on special effects but leave the plot to fend for itself.

If your plot isn't thickening, you're going to have watery sales.

A good example of a plot with unexpected twists is the movie Signs. *The movie was portrayed as an alien attack, a suspense thriller to keep teens up at night, but looking deeper into the plot, you find a story of a man who had lost his faith and, through the circumstances of aliens attacking his home, rediscovers his faith. The aliens were the catalyst, but they weren't the plot.*

Make your plots rich enough to disallow cheap theatrics. Your readers will know the difference, and the LDS market insists on a higher standard. Don't confuse this with thinking you can't put in any detail. We are supposed to show and not tell, and with practice, editing, and rewriting, you'll find the balance that will tantalize, yet not offend.

SCIENCE FICTION

[Tristi] When it comes to the LDS market, Science Fiction and Fantasy are new and emerging genres, even though they've been national bestsellers for decades. Few LDS publishers have wanted to risk producing speculative fiction until recently. And those who do have been very particular about the subject matter.

Why is this such a big problem?

It's a safe bet that there are hundreds and thousands of Church members out there who are avid Trekkies or *Star Wars* fans or *Lord of the Rings* movie die-hards. In addition, there are vast numbers of members who regularly read science fiction and fantasy novels. Their testimonies or basic understanding of the plan of salvation are not necessarily challenged by such far reaches into the unknown or impossible. It's just for fun. It's make-believe. It's entertaining and fascinating. We all understand that.

It's also a safe bet that many of those same folks also enjoy reading LDS fiction on occasion—even historical fiction, where minor events are created and words are put into the mouths of well-known scriptural figures. (Think of *The Work and the Glory* or *Tennis Shoes Among the Nephites.*) Testimonies aren't necessarily challenged by these stretches of the imagination, either.

The problem arises when the two are mixed into one forum, when doctrinal subjects become speculative, which I would term LDS Speculative Fiction. When the words "LDS" and "Speculative" are used in the same breath, hackles are raised, as well as eyebrows.

In this day and age, with the fullness of the gospel revealed, we all have a pretty good idea about what will occur in the future, who really lives out there in the deep recesses of outer space, and how our world will eventually end. By and large, we don't like it when those truths are challenged—even in the format of a make-believe, fictional book.

For instance, suppose you read a science fiction book about aliens from outer space who visit our world, select a few random earthlings from the downtown streets, and suck them up into their spaceship for scientific study. This is nothing out-of-bounds or unusual. There are numerous books, plays, and movies based on a similar premise.

But what if you get to chapter four, and you're suddenly made aware that two of the earthlings being studied by the six-legged Martian scientists are dressed in suits and white shirts and ties, with little black nametags fastened to their jacket pockets? Mormon missionaries on an alien spaceship? Hold on! All of a sudden you're mad. You slam the book shut in revulsion, and throw it across the room at the opposite wall—right over the trash can.

Why? Because you "know" this would never happen. Your knowledge and testimony of the gospel have been challenged, sacred things tinkered with, and "pearls cast to the swine," leaving a bad taste in your mouth. It seems sacrilegious.

Great care must be taken, when dealing with science fiction or fantasy, that the things you present are not misconstrued as sacrilege—and it *is* possible to accomplish this.

For example, in Linda Paulson Adams' book *Prodigal Journey*, the story is set in future times surrounding the second coming of Christ. This could be tricky business. But Linda expertly crafts a story, not about the Second Coming, but about two ordinary young people in love—who just happen to live during this eventful time in earth's history. As different things happen throughout the story, it's very easy to assimilate those things into the realm of "what might be" or "could happen," based on what we know and understand. Nothing really challenges our beliefs, even though great liberties are taken to invent possible scenarios, characters, and events—including an encounter with Christ Himself. It's all believable.

It's a fine line to tread, but it *can* be done successfully.

The other option, of course, is not to mix the two, and just stay away from mentioning the Church altogether, as James Dashner does in his popular new series, *The Jimmy Fincher Saga*.

It's pure science fiction, entirely out of the realm of normality, and yet thoroughly enjoyable and non-offensive. Dan Yates does a similar job with his *Angels* series, giving us a fun, tongue-in-cheek approach to the afterlife, without throwing in obvious doctrinal elements. Both authors are LDS, and their books have all sold successfully in the LDS market.

ROMANCE

Novel-length romantic fiction has become very popular in the LDS market. Let's envision your novel for a moment. You're on a roll. You have a great plot and compelling characters.

Let's take a peek at how you're doing.

Do you have a knock-out ending? It has to be happy, or it's not a "romance." This genre is well-defined and specific. There are certain rules and guidelines—such as the happy ending—which cannot be broken for the story to stay in the genre and please the romance reader.

In the LDS market, a host of additional rules apply to what your readers will tolerate when it comes to romantic interludes between your characters.

Take the following example:

> *Ron turned to face Christine. "You look beautiful tonight," he said, reaching toward her.*

How you proceed from this sentence forward will determine just how well you do in the LDS market. As Latter-day Saints, our code of complete chastity before marriage and total fidelity afterward sets us apart.

"But it wasn't going to be graphic!" you say. Explicit scenes clearly don't belong in an LDS romance. That's generally not the argument. Debate comes into play determining just what is acceptable, and what is not, in the so-called "gray areas." This is where it gets sticky. Each person has individual limits for what is offensive or too graphic. The writer may come up with something they feel is completely appropriate, yet a reader takes offense.

In my historical novel *Nothing to Regret*, the main character and his girlfriend become parents of an illegitimate child. This baby proves to be an important catalyst to the story—the reason for living that my main character so badly needs. But I wanted to downplay the scene where he and his girlfriend had intimate relations, and focus instead on the other issues at hand. I used the following words to describe that event:

> *She covered her face with her hands and began to cry. I wrapped her in my arms and held her, stroking her hair, kissing her face. She turned her lips up to meet mine and we kissed, at first gently, then passionately. A half hour later she climbed out of my bed and stood, saying, "I must leave."*

This is as close as I came to describing what actually took place. I didn't feel it was appropriate or necessary to say more or spell it out in detail. Even so, a few readers were still offended by what I wrote. One woman commented that she doesn't read books like that, and another said she was ready to put the book down when she came to that part.

I can understand their feelings. I would certainly never try to determine for someone else what they should think and feel. But from my perspective, this illegitimate child was necessary to the story, so it was necessary to bring up how it came into being.

Interestingly enough, when my friend Josi Kilpack read the book, she wasn't sure where the baby came from. My reference was so vague that she hadn't picked up on it—the same passage that had so greatly offended these other ladies. Go figure!

[Julie] After I read that scene, I also wondered where the baby came from. It was too quick for me to catch it. Not that I needed a big hot-and-heavy make-out scene, but I was a bit confused. This is a prime example of how every person is unique and will respond to things differently. Something that you consider innocent might be shocking and appalling to another person. And something you find shocking could be a walk in the park for someone else.

Tristi's portrayal was tastefully handled, and her protagonist's remorse later was real. It helped to make that scene acceptable.

[Rachel] In sticky situations like the one above, there will always be some people who will be offended. Always. The trick is to do as Tristi did, and make it as inoffensive as possible for the majority of people.

Some people might advise us to simply stop writing stories that have issues like this, but we can't. These things happen in real life, and for our stories to seem real—to be stories that readers will care about—we must mirror real life. The way Tristi handled the scene above was the only way she could have written it for the LDS market.

[Tristi] Whenever there is debate over the appropriateness of a book's content, the LDS publisher invariably gets caught in the middle. After all, they want to sell books that appeal to the largest possible audience. Sometimes they have to make tough editorial decisions that may rub the author the wrong way. It's not moral issues alone that force a publisher to cut scenes; it's the very real fact that if the reader is unpleasantly shocked, they will not continue to buy, which is bad for authors, publishers, and even LDS bookstores. But since you simply can't predict what will shock someone, it's a hard line to walk.

[Rachel] That's the truth. I have a friend whose publisher once raked her over the coals for the phrase, "His hand lingered near hers." We couldn't believe it! We're talking about hands *here! But the publisher had received some complaints, and for a while was ultra-sensitive to anything that might make someone—anyone—feel uncomfortable. My friend ended up compromising on a lot of issues, but still managed to kept his hand lingering near hers.*

[Tristi] So what do you do when the audience is clamoring for romance, for something that will send that warm—chaste—thrill down the spine? There's a huge market for romance. How do you satisfy that craving without breaking the rules of LDS publishing?

Let's go back to Ron and Christine for a minute.

> *Ron looked deep into Christine's eyes. "You look beautiful tonight," he said, reaching toward her. He traced the soft outline of her cheek with his finger. "I never thought I'd find a woman like you." Taking her hand in his, they turned toward the fountain. "Every drop of water looks like a diamond," he said. "Like this one." He pulled a ring from his pocket and held it up to the light. "What do you think? Is this as pretty as the water in the fountain?"*
>
> *"Prettier," she said with a gasp as he slid it on her finger.*
>
> *He pulled her into his arms and kissed her, feeling the warmth of her lips against his with a tingle he could only compare to electricity.*

So far, so good. We're satisfying the desire for romance without taking things too far.

> *He ran his hands through her hair as they kissed, feeling the silky strands sift through his fingers like sand. Nothing had ever felt so right as her closeness, knowing that she would soon be his forever. He slid his hands down her arms, pulling her closer, then reached around her waist until her soft form nestled against his chest.*

Okay, wait! We're starting to push the envelope here. One more description of how she feels against him, or if he moves his hands any farther, and we're done for. To be safe, I might even delete that last sentence altogether.

A great thing about literature is that fiction readers generally have wonderful imaginations. You can convey a sense of romance and intimacy without spelling everything out. You can drop enough hints that readers can dream up the rest if they like, and stay within the bounds of what the audience will accept.

[Julie] Tristi is right. People have wonderful imaginations and don't need to be patronized by a writer that refuses to let them use it.

Another thing to remember with romance is that the "warm tingle" doesn't have to come from physical interaction at all. In my novel Loved Like That, *the heroine and hero never even kiss. And yet the book is filled with all the spine tingling warmth of being in love. Some readers complained that they expected at least a kiss in the end, but others have said how pleased they were to find such a wonderful ending that was totally cheeseless and non cliché.*

The ending worked perfectly, and here's why: sometimes people don't have to kiss or make physical contact to show how they feel—if what they're feeling is real.

One of the most romantic dates I ever had in my life was when we went to a make-out point, crawled in the back seat of my car, and read The Forgotten Carols *by Michael McLean together. We played a song on my tape player at the end of each chapter. We were there for hours. We never kissed once. In spite of the lack of smooching in a very smoochy place, that night will stand out forever in my mind as a perfect, shivering, tingling, wow-I-am-in-love night.*

Consider this when you're writing. Think of Sleepless in Seattle*—a perfect romance, and not one kiss between the two of them in the whole movie. A skilled writer can make it work, if they put a little effort into it.*

[Rachel] One of the tests I put my romantic scenes through is whether or not it would be appropriate for my young daughters to read. Girls as young as eleven read LDS romances, and this is another reason we need to be very careful, yet at the same time cultivate realism. We don't want to inspire inappropriate emotions in girls that are too young, but neither do we want to paint a rosy hue over very real feelings. LDS women are looking for realism, and girls need to know that there are problems with relationships. Bad things do happen to nice people. Emotions can get out of control. This means that we need to either show restraint in our characters, or show the consequences of their mistakes. Regardless of the plot, we cannot be explicit.

LANGUAGE

[Tristi] LDS readers, for the most part, have made it clear that they want books to be free of profanity. An occasional swear word was once acceptable, but not any more. There has been a notable shift in the market in the past few years to avoid any type of profanity or vulgarity in LDS novels—especially if you're publishing with the larger publishers who have retail outlets and who are very aware of customer complaints and expectations. The smaller publishers have also tended to follow this trend.

A possible exception lies where there's a non-member involved. (Sure seems like those non-members get away with a lot, doesn't it?) Generally speaking, a non-member can let something slip from time to time, but they should make an effort to watch their mouths when they're around members, and they should never, *ever* take the Lord's name in vain. Some of the lesser swear words may make it in, but using the name of Deity will not be accepted, regardless of who says it or under what circumstances. Neither will vulgarity in any form. You should check with your publisher in regards to their house rules on swearing.

So what do you do if you want your character to swear, but don't want to use an actual word? Let's pretend for a moment that Clay, Christine's old boyfriend, has just found out that Christine is engaged to Ron. He's not one bit happy about it, and calls her to beg for forgiveness.

> *"Clay, it's over between us. I'm sorry, but you and I want different things in life. Ron is perfect for me, and I know I'll be very happy with him. Please don't call me again; it's too painful, for both of us."*
>
> *Clay held the dead receiver in his hand, hearing her words echo over and over in his mind. How could she be so cold? He had truly loved her, and he thought she loved him. Cursing aloud, he slammed down the phone.*

This is all that's needed in a case like this. The readers will fill in for themselves, using their own imagination.

Consider a historical novel where a mob is chasing Church members. You simply cannot have them shooting over their heads (to avoid the blood and murder we discussed earlier) and have them yell, "Oh, those darn Mormons!" Sorry, that just doesn't work. Some "mild" profanity may be necessary, but other descriptive options should really be explored first.

Keep your audience in mind and use your best judgement. If in doubt, leave it out. Sometimes trying to second-guess the LDS market can be a tricky and risky thing to do.

SHORT FICTION AND POETRY

[Rachel] Unfortunately, there's not much of a market for books of short stories or poetry. This is true, not just in the LDS market, but nationwide as well. If LDS-themed stories and poetry are your heart's desire, you should be aware that there are few places that will publish them as collections. Even Jack Weyland experienced a long-term challenge finding a publisher for his collection of short stories. That's not to say it couldn't happen, just that these things typically do not sell enough copies to be worth the financial risk a publisher takes on each book they produce.

But what if short fiction or epic verse is still your true love? Well, begin by giving it a better chance. Check out Chapter Three in this book on writing and submitting articles, where you'll find information on how to submit to periodicals and magazines. The rules for submitting short fiction and poetry are about the same.

If your book of poetry comes back rejected, this is likely not based on your writing skill, but on the market. It doesn't matter if you're a Mormon Milton or Shakespeare, it's a matter of sales and business. People simply don't buy short fiction or poetry in the amounts necessary to make it worth the printing, editing, and marketing costs.

Recently the Ensign, New Era, *and* Friend *magazines stopped publishing fiction at all. They might occasionally print a poem or two, but these are also rare, and submissions are often reserved for special contests. Check each magazine for guidelines on whether they accept fiction and poetry submissions, and how to send these in.*

Irreantum *and* Meridian *do accept fiction and poetry with LDS themes, or that are written by LDS writers. (Contact information for these and other LDS periodicals is listed in Chapter Three on* Articles.*)*

You could also try the many periodicals and contests listed in the Poet's Market *and* Novel and Short Story Writer's Market *if your work is aimed for a broader audience.*

NONFICTION

[Tristi] If you chronicle events that actually took place, you have more latitude with the subject matter you address.

For example, violence was a daily occurrence between the Saints and the Indians in the early days of the settlement of Utah. Lee Nelson's series *The Storm Testament* discusses scalpings and all sorts of things that are considered quite violent. He gets away with it because while it *is* fiction, the books describe actual events, or events similar to those that actually took place.

But he is still mindful of the audience and doesn't stray into graphic depictions.

A straight nonfiction book, *We Were Not Alone* by Karola Hilbert Reece, tells the story of an LDS family living in Germany during World War II. This family endured many difficult things during the war, including the near-molestation of their daughters. Because the book is factual, it is tolerated in the LDS market. Were these things written as fiction, they would not be as easily accepted.

[Rachel] I agree with Tristi. If the above-mentioned scenes had been fiction, they would have to be much more carefully written to be accepted in this market.

And to reiterate Tristi's comment on not being too graphic, remember that nonfiction doesn't give the writer a license to portray unnecessary details. The girls in We Were Not Alone *came very close to being abused, but we still don't need a line-by-line narrative of every little detail.*

When writing my novel A Heartbeat Away*, which was inspired by many national kidnapping cases, I had to be very careful in portraying how the kidnapper attacked his young victim. It didn't matter that in real life, kidnapping victims are often raped repeatedly, tortured, and killed in various horrific ways. I didn't need to go into detail to bring out the fear my character felt:*

> *He pushed me back into the rough, sandy dirt. I fought him with all my might, careless of the pain, but that only seemed to urge him on. I was so scared and mad and sad all at once. And also glad that Meghan wasn't here. This would have destroyed her. But I was strong. I would fight. In determination, I scratched at his neck. He answered with a fist to my jaw that made bright pinpoints of light echo in my skull.*
>
> *When I couldn't fight anymore, he began to do things to me. I was ashamed and glad for the darkness, even though I knew none of it was my fault. There was a lot of pain, but that was just the beginning.*
>
> *Months before when I heard on the news about a child dying from a beating from his own parents I had said to my mom. "Don't you think that God took away his pain so he didn't feel them hurting him?"*
>
> *I'll always remember the look on my mother's face as she sat very still, pondering my question. Her blue eyes seemed bluer and turned inward, as though searching deeply. "I think," she began after a very long while, "that we don't really understand a lot of things. This life is so short. The pain that baby felt, while very terrible—unacceptable—was also very short. And it is that pain and suffering that will stand as a testimony against those people on Judgment Day." She sighed. "I really don't know the*

answer, honey, but I do know that whatever that baby felt, or what any innocent person feels when they suffer, will eventually be swallowed by the love of Christ in the life to come."

Well, I can tell you that I felt what my kidnapper did to me. Every sickening little bit. I thought at any minute I would die from the pain that seemed to go on and on in wave after wave of agony.

That was as far as I could go to depict realism while still retaining my LDS readership. Note the break in the attack as the girl thinks about the baby on the news. This puts a little distance between my reader and this unthinkable act of violence, and also justifies my reasons as an author for including even this brief description of her pain. What follows after is quite different (my character's experience with the afterlife), allowing readers to recover and feel joy again.

The bottom line is that, either with fiction or nonfiction, we must use care with the portrayal of all our difficult scenes.

PUSHING THE ENVELOPE

[Tristi] Most books can handle one or two scenes where the author pushes the envelope, then backs away. Ron and Christine might get away with a passionate kiss by the fountain. A few drops of blood might make their way into a mystery or thriller. But be careful.

For instance, suppose we prolonged that kiss by the fountain. Ron takes Christine home and walks into the apartment with her. They turn on the light to find Christine's roommate Monica lying in a pool of blood in the middle of the room. If we've described the kiss with lots of detail, and then describe that blood with lots of detail, that's probably more than the market will bear. Decide what's most important, then don't play it up too much. Sex sells in the world, but this is one market where sex does not sell.

This doesn't mean that your options are limited. It may seem that way, knowing that you have to choose your words carefully.

Sometimes it may seem unfair that you have to change what you've written in order to please these faceless people who will someday read your book. You can't control what they like anyway, right? True. But it pays in the long run to pay attention to market trends. You may be writing for the love of writing, but you do want to make some money, at least enough for your publisher to want to keep publishing your work—or at least buy ink or toner for your printer!

Sometimes authors either write for art or for publication. In many cases the two cannot coexist. If you write for publication, you must know what your market wants and give it to them. Being an LDS author means you can write for publication without compromising your own standards, and that in turn becomes your art.

When you screen out from your writing those things that might give offense, you find the opportunity to reach into a vast reservoir of words to create an experience of beauty for your reader. As mentioned before, you can plant in your reader's mind a picture so real and so vivid that you can drop the merest hint, and they will know exactly what happens next.

The beauty of it is that in every reader's mind the scene will be different, the "what happens next" will be different, and you have created a thousand possible stories living in the hearts and imaginations of a thousand different people.

Down the road, as you master your craft, the chance to break out of the LDS market and go national might come along. If you have attained a good following in the LDS market—largely by staying true to their standards and expectations—you will look very attractive to national agents and publishers. (Maybe even as good as Christine looked to Ron!) Since you are successful in your own genre, they are more likely to take you on and see what else you can do. You will gain a readership that will span the population of the country, not just LDS readers. At that point you might think you can write what you like without the restrictions of the LDS realm.

A word of caution, though. As you go national, your LDS readers may go with you to see what you write next. If you stray too far from LDS guidelines, you may lose the respect of those readers—and they might choose not to read your work anymore, even those books written for the LDS market.

[Julie] Don't mind my little Jiminy Cricket voice here, but you also have a degree of respect you need to maintain. Sometimes self respect cannot be bartered away for the price tag on a garish, bloody murder scene or a sex scene that leaves nothing to the imagination.

If you plan on going national, make certain you outline your limits of what is and is not acceptable to you. After creating your boundaries, stick with them.

In an acting class I had, my teacher explained the need for us to set our standards now so that when a contract was handed to us with an obscene amount of money being offered, we didn't compromise ourselves for a price.

The same can be true for writing.

Don't feel you need to cater to the perceived wants of a national market in order to succeed. By setting your standards now, you will be able to maintain that level of self-respect and dignity that you demand of yourself. Though it may at first appear that LDS writers in the national market are hiding who they are and what they believe under a pen name, some choose to use a pen name for marketability.

For myself, I have a chosen pen name that I plan to use for the books that I will write for the national market.

I did not choose a pen name so that I could hide my standards and write about raucous debauchery and sin, but simply because Julie Wright isn't exactly marketable as a name. I love my name, but it doesn't really ring. My standards are carried throughout my writing regardless of whether or not the piece is meant for the national market.

I confess to being more light-handed with what I put into my nationally-intended books than with what I put into my LDS fiction, but not so much that my LDS readers would feel scandalized if they stumbled onto a book under my pen name.

Regardless of where I intend to publish, I couldn't write an explicit sex scene (I'd be blushing too much) nor could I write a scene with the graphic details of a brutal murder. These are elements that honestly don't entertain me, and I feel that if I can't entertain myself when I write, then I am helpless to entertain anyone else.

[Rachel] I agree completely that you need to decide now what you will or won't write—even for the national market. I'm headed in that direction myself, and while there are many things I feel good about writing for the national market that wouldn't make it in the LDS market, I think it's vital to maintain our personal standards.

WHEN A CHARACTER STRAYS

[Tristi] As seen in some of the examples above, we can't always avoid difficult circumstances in our LDS books. What do you do if your character has strayed—physically or spiritually? In order for this to be acceptable in the eyes of the LDS readership, the character must have consequences. The following are examples:

1. A character is disfellowshipped or excommunicated from the Church.
2. A character feels deep sorrow for sins, repents, and turn his or her life around. (And make sure the straying scenes aren't too graphic!)
3. If a character has suffered a loss of testimony, he or she finds it before the end of the book.
4. Sometimes the "strayer" could be the "bad guy" or a minor character, and the main character helps them work through the problem.

It's amazing how many lives have been touched by reading a book about the power of the Atonement. As a character makes a mistake, then finds grace and forgiveness from the Savior, the readers can feel the strength of that forgiveness in their own hearts, and testimonies can be strengthened as they read.

If your character isn't a member of the Church yet, serious transgressions can be more easily forgiven by your readers. Maybe the character has a "past," comes into contact with the Church, and repents. LDS readers will forgive a sinning non-member a lot faster than they will a member who strays.

A perfect example is found in *Nothing to Regret*, when Ken comes in contact with the Church for the first time. He was unaware that intimacy with his girlfriend was wrong. His parents had taught him to wait until he was in love—and he truly was.

But when he meets the missionaries and learns about the law of chastity, his heart is broken as he realizes that he has broken one of the Lord's cardinal commandments. He suffers deeply as he seeks forgiveness for everything he has done contrary to the will of the Lord. He is forgiven and is baptized into the Church, and later receives his temple endowments and marries in the temple.

Because Ken was a non-member at the time of his sin, it was easier for my audience to accept what he had done. Several of my readers have made the comment, "Well, he wasn't a member of the Church at the time. He didn't know any better." As they saw Ken bear the difficult burden of remorse for his sins and repent, the readers were able to forgive him. The reader's forgiveness of a sinning character is something to strive for; you want the reader to feel compassion and sympathy for your character so they will want to know more about them—what happens next. Many of my readers have asked for a sequel.

Another warning—a hallmark of LDS literature is weaving gospel principles throughout the story. Yet readers can't stand being preached to throughout the book. With my character Ken, it was best to show the consequences of sin and the blessings of obedience through the character's actions rather than to lecture on doctrine.

GETTING ACCEPTED BY STORES

When an LDS book rolls off the press, and sometimes before, the publisher sends a sample copy to Deseret Book and to Seagull Book and Tape. They review it for market appropriateness. If they feel it falls within the proper guidelines, and that it will sell reasonably well, they will agree to carry it in their stores. This is very important for your book, for the following reasons:

1. Approval sends the message that it's a worthwhile book. Your book passed a rigorous and demanding review process and was found acceptable.
2. Approval attracts readers. If LDS readers know your book has been approved, they feel safe in buying it, knowing it won't contain anything objectionable.
3. Approval convinces other stores to carry your book. Deseret Book and Seagull set the trends. If your book is approved by them, other stores will want to carry it, too.
4. Disapproval puts an automatic black mark on your book and possibly your name. There's a strong chance many LDS readers won't want anything to do with it.

If Deseret Book and Seagull refuse to carry your book, you have other options. Some independent bookstores may stock it for you. You can also list your title on Amazon.com, you can create a website and sell it there, and so on. But without the two major stores backing you up, you may have a difficult road ahead of you.

Still, if you want to be an LDS author, and write stories that inspire and uplift Latter-day Saints, it only makes sense to use good judgment in your content. Despite the transgression my character committed in *Nothing to Regret*, the book was accepted by Deseret Book and Seagull and became part of their inventory. Its messages of the Atonement, repentance, and forgiveness, are woven into the story.

I'm grateful that these two fine stores chose to recognize the story for what it was.

Have fun, be creative, and be mindful of your boundaries. As you do this, you gain a readership that knows they can trust you and will eagerly look forward to reading your next book.

The Truth Shall Set You Free

WRITING NON-FICTION

by Linda Shelley Whiting

with contributions by
Tristi Pinkston & Shirley Bahlmann

When writing non-fiction for the LDS market, the choice of subject is probably the most important decision you will make. I always make this a matter of prayer.

CHOOSING A SUBJECT

[Tristi] Ask yourself these questions: "Which figures in Church history have been the most inspirational to you? Does a story about an early saint or prophet make you long to dig deeper and discover more about that person?" Take a moment to think about what aspects of that era mean the most to you. As a teenager I traveled to many Church history sites and stood where Joseph Smith once stood. That was a profound and moving experience for me—one that will someday find its way into a book.

[Shirley] Your subject needs to intrigue you, to capture your mind and heart. You will spend a lot of time with it, so be sure you like its company!

THE RESEARCH

[Linda W] Unless you have unpaid, working graduate students at your disposal, you might find yourself spending five to ten years researching and writing about your topic, whether it's a history of an event or the definitive biography of a major Church figure. Norma B. Ricketts spent over ten years researching and writing her award-winning book, *The Mormon Battalion: U.S. Army of the West, 1846-1848.*

Consider reading *How to Write: Advice and Reflections* by Richard Rhodes. This is a great book on how to write history. He is also the best-selling author of *The Making of the Atom Bomb.* Rhodes believes taking notes in libraries is a waste of time. He advocates copying sections of manuscripts and reference books (which cannot be checked out) that may have source material, and doing careful analysis of the information gleaned when you get home.

[Tristi] Of course, if the book is available for checkout, I take it home with me. That way I have the opportunity to look it over thoroughly. Plus there are copyright issues with copying pages of books that are available for checkout.

[Linda W] It is imperative to read the nonfiction guidelines of LDS publishers, which are generally available on their websites. You need to know what potential publishers want. Many (Deseret Book, Covenant, Greg Kofford Books) require copies of all the pages cited in endnotes or footnotes, so they can check the research without leaving their offices. Knowing this ahead of time, and making those copies as you research, will save you time and frustration down the road.

A good starting point is a database. A number of good LDS historical CD databases came out in the 1990s, including LDS Historical Library, InfoBase Collectors Library, and GospeLink. InfoBase Library was meshed into GospeLink in recent years. As of 2004, the latter was still available at deseretbook.com for around $70. It has also become an on-line service.

If possible, find a friend or acquaintance who has a copy of one of these, and download information on your subject to a disc. Print this out and make a list of every book and manuscript that mentions your topic. If your focus is too modern or too obscure for these databases, pick the best-documented book you can find, and use its bibliography as your starting list. A little at a time, bring each of these books to your local public library through interlibrary loan and copy all the sections that involve your area of interest. The footnotes of these books will cite other sources. You can then make a new list and send for more books. For a good researcher, this process can seem almost never-ending.

[Shirley] When your subject captivates you, the time spent immersed in research is like a treasure hunt. When I read old documents from pioneer days, it feels like I'm taking a walk through a field of grass with the sun shining, a breeze rustling the leaves, and a blanket of contentment settled around my shoulders. A paragraph catches my eye, and it's as though a jack rabbit jumped up from hiding in the tall grass and zigzags through the field. My eyes widen, my heart quickens, and I reread the account that I know will become a story in my book. I've struck gold!

[Linda W] Any book on regular library shelves (not reference books or special collections) in nearly any public or university library is available to you through interlibrary loan. The national interlibrary loan system is a researcher's dream. Most libraries in the country—with the exception of some smaller rural libraries—join in this consortium to share books.

This means that almost any book published within the last 100 years or so is available to you, since a copy can usually be found somewhere in some library in America. The service is normally free, although some small libraries charge a nominal fee. Even private universities like Brigham Young University, Harvard, and Columbia are in the system.

It's simple to use. Just go to your nearest public library and ask the librarian what forms to fill out. When your books arrive, the library calls, and you take them home for three weeks. Many large city library systems also offer interlibrary loan online.

[Shirley] I live in rural Utah, and I use interlibrary loan quite frequently. In my world, it's like getting birthday presents all year long. It's magic!

[Linda W] Microfilmed newspapers can also be ordered through this service. These are usually free, but occasionally they require a small fee of less than ten dollars. If you don't know the name of the newspaper, but you know the town and approximate time period, librarians can help you look in the right places to find the exact title. While in the process of ordering these books, make a list of all the manuscripts that are mentioned in the database.

You can check online to see if any of these are in Brigham Young University's Special Collections. BYU is wonderful about giving access to scholars. When you make a trip to BYU or another large library, rather than reading each manuscript, flip through fast, find the sections that might involve your subject, and copy all those pages for later study. Yes, the copying bill is huge, but wisdom rules this madness. It is much easier to study these journals carefully at home. It's also more economical, especially if you don't live in Utah. If you ask for sensitive records, such as the transcript of Joseph Smith's trial at Far West, the head of Special Collections may come out and talk with you. Be honest and open, and let him know you have no desire to harm the Church. Once the Special Collections librarians know your subject, they often suggest additional records that may contain useful information.

Make a point of getting to know the librarians in all the libraries you use. They are valuable allies in your search for truth.

In most special collections, the reading room is a separate area, watched by staff. Only a minimum amount of notebooks or paper is permitted, and no ink pens are allowed. If you are reading old, original records, the staff might ask you to wear white gloves so the oils from your skin won't damage the documents. What you view in the reading room is often only a copy of the original, as many documents are previously copied or microfilmed.

Our country has many great libraries. You might need to visit quite a few to read everything available on your subject. For example, to write a book on the Mormon settlement of Arizona, you would need to use the Church Historian's Office and BYU. The next step would be to check the special collections in the major public libraries of Mesa and Phoenix, Arizona State University, Northern Arizona University, and University of Arizona. All these libraries have manuscripts on early Arizona Mormons, which are not available anywhere else.

The LDS Church Archives is housed at the Church Historian's Office (CHO), located in the Church Office Building near Temple Square in Salt Lake City. Unlike BYU and other university special collections, the Church Archives does not allow material to be photocopied unless you are a direct descendant of the person you're researching, but pencils and typewriters are available, and they do allow laptop computers. Copying records this old-fashioned way takes time. It took me a full week to write out David Patten's missionary journal in longhand.

The CHO will interview scholars when they first arrive. Expect to be questioned again if you request delicate records. In recent years, the CHO has been betrayed by those whose motives were to discredit the Church, so they are naturally very cautious. Don't be frightened by the questioning. If you are a serious scholar and a Church member in good standing, you should have no problem receiving access to most records.

Computers on the premises contain the catalog for the Archives. One valuable part of the Archives is their collection of old photographs, prints of which can be purchased for use in your book. The cost is $10 per print, or $5 per digital copy on CD. You must write the Church Copyright and Permissions Office for permission to use them. This appears to be a formality in most cases, but you should not neglect it.

Another library system not to be overlooked by historical authors is the LDS Family History Library, with its branches throughout the world.

[Tristi] The Internet is another valuable tool for research. I am constantly amazed how many websites come up when I do a search on my topic of interest. One thing I learned the hard way, though (and this goes for the Internet and every other form of research), is that it's critical—even vital—to double-check your information. Internet data is not known for being accurate or complete.

The huge amount of research required to write a good history may seem overwhelming, but it is well worth every moment. If you dislike research, or would rather not invest quite as much time, an alternative for you might be historical fiction. This still demands dedication and hard work, but not so much as for a nonfiction history. When I write a historical fiction novel, I may spend weeks or months rather than years doing research.

THE WRITING PROCESS

[Linda W] Writing a history or biography is not like eating a piece of chocolate cheesecake. It's tough, hard work.

[Shirley] Take heart! It's work worth doing and is ultimately satisfying. At the end, you'll be glad you built the cheesecake factory, instead of settling for just one piece.

[Linda W] Before you begin writing, you need to read through all of your material at *least* once. Develop your theme. Then make an outline that ties together all the events of the person's life. The one most often used is to go in chronological order, from birth to death.

[Shirley] Yet some writers choose to start their books with a significant, attention-grabbing event in their subject's history, and then go back later to review their earlier life.

[Linda W] Start with the first section of the outline and lay out all the copied pages from journals and book sections. You may find you have six to ten versions of each event. Read them over and over.

Think about your approach to the event, and do your best to determine what is true and what is false in your sources. Making these decisions of truth correctly is what being a good historian is all about.

This is no simple matter.

Just because someone wrote something in a journal does not make it true. People lied in the 1800s the same as they do now. Also personal perceptions, and a myriad of other reasons, can cloud why a person wrote what they did. When you read these records, pray for the gift to discern the truth. In *David W. Patten*, I needed to write about Mormon Militiaman Gideon Carter, who died at the site of the Battle of Crooked River and was left behind by mistake among the enemy casualties. After the Missourians took care of their dead and wounded, the Mormons went back and retrieved him.

I had four or five accounts of his body finally being brought to Far West in a wagon. Some were from the Mormon point of view, and some were from an anti-Mormon perspective. One pro-Mormon account said his eyes were gouged out and that the Missourians had hacked up his body with corn knives. The other three sources didn't mention this mutilation.

So what really happened? I questioned the mutilation, since the other sources didn't mention it, including those written by Mormons. And also because of the words "corn knife." From previous reading, I knew that when apostates made up stories about the Danites, they often mentioned corn knives. This was an inflammatory phrase of the period, and meant a horrible, inhuman weapon. Also, I felt in my soul it just wasn't true. I sensed that this good brother, writing in his journal, hated the Missourians so much for killing his friend that he embellished on the horrors committed to Carter's body.

[Shirley] I had an interesting experience with my research. I interviewed Quay Hansen, the grandson of a subject for one of my stories, who gave his grandfather's name as Frank Joseph Hansen. When I got home, I realized that I needed the name of one of Frank's brothers to complete my story, so I got on the

Internet and logged on to the Family Search Internet Genealogy Service site. I found a man named Frank Hansen in the proper time frame and in the proper location. I printed out the information and laid it aside. It sat there virtually untouched for two days while I searched for the information that I needed to complete the story.

A few days later, for no apparent reason, I went back to the genealogy site and felt as though I should reverse the man's first and middle names. I typed in Joseph Frank Hansen. Of the many entries that came up, my eyes fastened on the name Joseph Franklin Hansen. "That's him," I heard myself murmur. I printed out his information, found his brother's name, and started writing the story.

Then I stopped myself. I thought I really should run this past Quay before I proceed further. I gave him a call, and he verified that his grandfather's name really was Joseph Franklin. He went by his middle name, Frank, so Quay had forgotten the proper order of his names until I brought it up.

[Linda W] Once you have determined what is most likely true, write out your version of the event, using details from all the various sources. Be careful to attribute each line, paragraph, or section to the correct source.

[Tristi] This goes along with what I said about checking your sources. What if Linda had only read one account of the Gideon Carter incident? What if she hadn't read enough to know about the nature of the term "corn knife"?

By using several sources, she was able to piece together a better idea of what probably happened. Yes, it can make your research more time-consuming, but wouldn't you rather have an accurate idea than a quick one?

[Shirley] That reminds me of a story I wrote about a little boy taken captive by an Indian chief. I found four or five accounts of the same story, and they all differed in the details—from the mother's name and the length of time the toddler was gone, to

the reason the boy was taken. I got to the point where I wished heartily that I could find an account from one of the boy's parents rather than word-of-mouth stories and legends passed down through generations.

My point is that if you're interested in history and nonfiction writing, you do future researchers a great favor when you keep written records of your own.

[Linda W] Finally, rewrite, rewrite, rewrite—and rewrite some more. Try to make it read smoothly, where one idea leads to another, very much like a novel might read. The creative juices flow during this phase for the historical writer. Many of the same writing skills that make great fiction also make great historical works.

[Tristi] Rewriting is one of my least favorite things, but I learn so much from the process.

[Shirley] I love to rewrite! The structure is already there, so all I have to do is paint and wallpaper and rearrange the flowers. There are times when I have to move a window or change the living room from the north side of the house to the south. That takes more brain power to blend the seams of the architecture, but I still enjoy the process.

[Tristi] What a great attitude, Shirley! I might have to borrow it.

[Linda W] It takes writing skill to avoid generalizations and to use as much specific, concrete detail as possible. Make your descriptions come alive by using all the senses: smell, sound, sight, taste, and touch.

The big difference between writing fiction and a history is that all the specifics have to be true. They can't be fabricated. The trick is to hunt for this color and flavor while you research facts of the events. If you discover your subject stood by a cypress tree, or the weather was rainy, or that the night smelled of orange blossoms, underline that detail in your copy, and make a note to yourself in the margin—USE THIS. Such seemingly insignificant details are what make the book come alive and set it apart from a dry college textbook.

Another tool to increase the power of your work is to use vibrant action verbs and avoid adverbs (words ending in *-ly*, also words like *just* and *very*). Be creative with your descriptions. Find ways to mold your words to present the reader's mind with a vivid picture *without* relying on adverbs.

[Tristi] Clichés ought to be avoided as well. I love an unusual sentence—one that relies on the writer's own sense of the world—instead of expressions that are chronically overused.

[Linda W] Having a good mix of simple and complex sentence structures within a paragraph also increases readability. It is wise to have another writer friend critique your work before you send it to a publisher, so it is as perfect as you can make it. A number of fine LDS writer critique groups have a presence on the Internet. A good group for LDS women is the American Night Writers' Association (ANWA).

[Tristi] I can't express how valuable it is to have a friend read your work for you—one who isn't afraid to be honest. It is through criticism that I learn to become a better writer.

[Shirley] Yes! Realize that honest feedback comes because the person cares enough to want your book to be the best that it can be, and be grateful that they love you enough to want you to have a fantastic book associated with your name.

[Linda W] Great historical writing can be just as interesting as fiction. Here's an example of descriptive writing from my favorite historical author, Juanita Brooks:

> *Jacob looked around with a heavy heart. The curled leaves of the corn rattled, the wilted stalks drooped in the center. The squash vines sprawled,*

> *their stems and leaves lying flat in wilted abandon on the ground. In the mesquite tree nearby a locust sang shrilly. A lizard scurried from the shelter of one bush to another, where he gingerly held up one foot after another from the burning sand. If rain were to do any good it must come soon.* Jacob Hamblin, pg. 51.

What she is describing here is not fabricated—it is true. Although she was not there with Hamblin, she did live in the region, and she had seen a garden in a drought and even a lizard lift its feet from the burning sand. She describes seeing the latter in her autobiography.

WRITING A SELF-HELP BOOK

[Tristi] Life has a way of teaching us lessons. It seems like each one of us has different obstacles to overcome. At the end of a trial, we look back on all we've learned in the process and naturally want to share it with others. We often do that, informally, when we find out a friend or family member is going through the same thing. (Okay, they don't often listen, but at least we try!)

You may want to take it even a step further and write a book about your experiences. There are a few trials in my life over which I'm anxiously waiting to triumph, so I can turn them all into best-selling books.

[Shirley] Now, if we all had that attitude about our trials, we would be set for a gloriously happy life!

[Tristi] For instance, my husband has recently changed to an alkalarian diet. That means eating foods without a lot of natural acids, which help instead to neutralize acid levels in your body. Therefore: no chocolate, no cheese, no fun stuff (which is why I haven't tried it yet). I plan to write a cookbook called "How to Cook For The Person Who Can't Eat Anything." Of course, first I have to figure it out myself.

[Shirley] Tristi reminds me of an important point. Even if you write nonfiction or how-to books, the title needs to be a creative attention-getter. A cookbook for someone who literally can't eat is a waste of time. That person won't last long enough for the book to be of any real use. Yet Tristi's title piques interest, and you are curious to pick up the book because you want to know more.

[Tristi] To write a self-help book, it's easier if you have personal knowledge of the situation, professional experience in your field, or are close to someone who has "been there, done that." Even though it may be more difficult to attempt a project of this kind without inside knowledge, if you're passionate about the topic, you can always research it and conduct interviews to accomplish your purpose.

[Shirley] If you have no personal knowledge, yet you feel compelled to write about a subject, you can do your best research and write up a draft. Then be sure to have at least one person who is familiar with that topic read through what you've written and check it for accuracy.

Maybe the book you've put together only has a section or two that deals with something you're unfamiliar with. You still want to have a person well-versed in that subject look it over and approve the information. After all, inaccurate writing will discredit your entire book and make you look like a fool. You can write it, but you want to do it right.

[Tristi] I strongly encourage writers to hit libraries, bookstores, and the Internet to find other books on the market that deal with your topic. For instance, many books have been published in the LDS market recently covering dating, marital intimacy, humor, help for parents, and so on. Before you put too much work into it, find out if it's already been done. If it has, could you put a new spin on it, make it fresher, more up to date?

[Linda W] Even with a lifetime of experience, if you have no medical or academic credentials of your own, you need to use research from those who do have them that support your ideas.

Better yet, obtain a first-hand interview from experts with credentials. Many readers only respect the opinion of someone with formal training. Whether fair or not, it's true. When you include professionals in your work, your personal experience supports their research, and is then more likely to be accepted.

In addition, most LDS publishers (or national publishers, for that matter) will not even look at a nonfiction manuscript that has no source material or professional background. They won't risk it. They have to consider the possibility that you might be wrong. If they publish something terribly incorrect, then *they* look silly and unreliable, and could lose their credibility in the market—all because they published your book. Publishers will not do any research to verify your angle. They won't take the time; they don't have it to spare. They'll just reject your manuscript. End of story.

You may, of course, choose to ignore wisdom and self-publish a book that lacks professional opinion, but you run a very real risk that readers will not believe you have anything useful to say without some type of professional support, and you may find yourself out a significant financial investment for a large stack of books that no one dares to buy.

Also, if your topic has been treated three or four times recently, publishers may not want to go there again just yet, or divide their marketing dollars between two or more books on the same topic. Bookstores may not want to give up shelf space, either, for yet another book on dating by an unknown author when those other three by General Authorities, CES officials, or renowned LDS figures are still selling beautifully.

[Tristi] This doesn't mean don't try! I've read many self-help books over the years, and the most useful to me have been the ones that incorporated personal stories, instead of clinical trials with faceless, nameless people. As you lay out the framework for your book, think about interviewing others who have endured the same trial, to get different perspectives on the issue. Maybe one of your readers won't see the problem the same way you did, but if they read your friend Betty Jo's comments, they may identify with her and understand how the things you say are useful to them as well.

Expression of feelings is crucial in this genre to help your reader to understand that you truly do understand, because you've been there or someone close to you has. When a reader seeks out and buys a self-help book, it's often because they need validation to know they are not alone, and hope to find answers that will make a difference in their lives. Don't be afraid to share your innermost thoughts. When it's just too personal—when you don't want your friends or family to know—you can give yourself a pseudonym and add yourself to the list of people you interviewed. This way you maintain anonymity while sharing your thoughts and feelings. Say you wrote a book about weight loss. (Keep a lookout—when I have this one conquered, I'll be writing one!) You feel it's useful to share a story of a time you were ridiculed, but are hesitant to broadcast it. For example:

> *Sometimes it's hard for an overweight person to receive the respect and positive attention they deserve. They feel invisible or sometimes even shunned because of their appearance. Lori, a 27-year-old stay-at-home mom, shared this experience:*
>
> *"I went to the store one day in sweats, with no makeup on. I felt a little embarrassed, like I should have taken the time to put myself together, but it was a crazy day—I was lucky I got a shower. I prayed I wouldn't run into anyone I knew. Then I realized . . . no one was looking at me anyway. I was the fat woman; I was invisible. It didn't matter if I wore makeup or not. No one paid me any attention."*

I have often had this feeling as an overweight woman. But in my eventual book on the topic, I might present it using the above method. I use my own persona as the narrative voice, and then quote myself using the pseudonym "Lori." This shares my emotions without feeling like a huge spotlight is focused on me, revealing every little flaw. It frees me to focus on the task at hand—writing the book.

[Linda W] Some self-help books seem to lack genuine honesty about the trials and hardships in the lives of those who strive to live the gospel on a day-to-day basis. If you want to create permanent change with real-life issues, it is imperative that you don't gloss over honest feelings of anger, hatred, loneliness, ecstasy, or the need for human kindness that are apparent in the lives of so many.

[Tristi] Present the information in a positive, upbeat way. Readers come to you with the hope that you can make them feel better. Reassure, reinforce, and keep in mind that they need validation. They need to know that their feelings are normal, that you've had them, too, and that there's nothing wrong with feeling depressed or anxious about the situation. Then go on to offer the encouragement and uplifting words they need.

[Shirley] Be sure you're in the proper frame of mind to address your subject. It's a proven fact that humor is beneficial, so I second Tristi's point that you've got to be upbeat and positive after the empathy part, so that your readers are uplifted. No one wants a book that is merely full of problems and recriminations.

[Tristi] The most important part of your book may be the chapter or chapters where you share with the reader the important role that the gospel played in your life, as you worked through this problem. The Spirit plays such a vital role in our lives as we try to overcome bad habits, deal with abuse, move on after divorce, or any other issue we may face. Our close contact with the Lord can buoy us up and carry us through challenges we never thought we could survive. Your reader will appreciate hearing how your own testimony was strengthened, perhaps even challenged, as you moved through your obstacle. Once again, it gives them something to identify with, a way for them to realize that they are not alone. It also makes your book more appealing to LDS publishers, who want to print books that inspire and uplift their audience.

However, do not artificially plant mentions of the Church throughout your book in the hope that it will catch the publisher's eye and get pushed to the forefront. Penelope Stokes, best-selling Christian novelist, stated that you should never try to write about a principle or belief which you do not personally espouse. Your reader will pick up on your lack of conviction, and your writing will appear false and plastic. Make sure you have a testimony of what you write before you write it. If you didn't happen to have a particularly spiritual experience while facing your trial, don't try to write an invented one into your book. However, I find it nearly impossible to write without a spiritual experience of some kind or another!

WRITING LDS DOCTRINE

[Tristi] In no other genre is a testimony of the gospel as important as it is when writing doctrine for the LDS market. A testimony is the strongest motivating factor for moving into this field; I can't imagine someone wanting to write a doctrinal book without feeling strongly about the subject matter.

As I cautioned in the section on self-help, be sure that what you're writing is a principle which you yourself strongly believe. If you try to insert spirituality where none exists naturally, the reader will pick up on a false tone and be unwilling to believe you, regardless of how well-meaning you may be.

The doctrinal genre is usually undertaken by Apostles, General Authorities, professional seminary teachers, religion professors, and others who spend large amounts of time teaching the Gospel. For these people, teaching has become a central part of their everyday lives. They devote much research and careful study of the scriptures to illustrate points and prove their theories. This is not reserved only for those who hold or held high positions in the Church, but in order to succeed with such an endeavor, you need to be willing to undertake the careful reading and introspection that it takes to bring about a good doctrinal book.

[Linda W] With so many books in existence about aspects of Church doctrine, especially the Atonement of Christ, in order for your book to be accepted by a publisher (and readers), you'll need a new and original idea on how the particular doctrine (which does not change) applies to life today. Your new idea, though, cannot be *new doctrine.* Writers must therefore be humble and very prayerful not to cross this line.

The Genuine Article

Making a Name in Periodicals

by Anne Bradshaw

with contributions by
Shirley Bahlmann & Linda Shelley Whiting

"But I don't like publicity," I said, in response to a helpful comment from my friend. "Can't I simply write books and leave the rest to a publisher? Surely LDS readers will watch out for good, clean novels?"

"You don't understand," came the reply. "Unless someone tells them you're out there, the public rarely discovers you. Like it or not, you have to find a way to make your name better known."

After chewing over this for a day, I came to the conclusion that it is ridiculous to waste all the effort and hours of writing books, only to find that few seek them because they've never heard of the author. I swallowed hard and decided it was time for action.

This section will look at writing for the LDS periodicals market—one of many roads to publicity. I chose this route because my writing career commenced many years ago when the *New Era* magazine for LDS youth accepted my submissions about Church members in England.

[Shirley] Periodical writing definitely works for getting your name known. I wrote books while my husband earned a name for himself as an award-winning sports writer for our local newspaper. I found that when I introduced myself as Shirley Bahlmann, people would nod as they responded, "Oh, Bahlmann."

My ego would puff up, as I was certain they recognized the name from one of my books. But then they continued, "Are you related to Bob Bahlmann who writes for the newspaper?" My bubble would burst, and my swelled head would shrink back to the right size for hiding under my hat.

[Linda W] Another reason to write for periodicals is for the personal connections you can make. The LDS publishing world is small enough that many writers, editors, and typesetters know each other, so there is crossover between the periodicals and book worlds. Two examples: Valerie Holladay, once a top book editor at Covenant, is now at Ancestry Inc., where she edits books and works as a contributing editor for their magazine Ancestry. *Marny Parkin typesets books for Cedar Fort, Inc., BYU Studies, and other journals, and is a contributing editor for* Irreantum *literary magazine.*

Writing articles helps authors make friends in the industry, which can aid in promoting future books. I write freelance for the Arizona Beehive, *an LDS newspaper, so when my book about David W. Patten came out, the* Beehive *editor was willing to interview me about the book in their paper—great publicity.*

Another benefit to publishing articles is that book editors will take your manuscript more seriously when you can list familiar magazines in which your work has been published.

[Anne] With this in mind, let's take a look at the required ingredients for an article that sparkles enough to get accepted. After discussing basics, I'll share a few secrets to help you begin submitting manuscripts. Remember that magazine editors are busy people, preferring fast information in an understandable and easy-to-remember format. Articles that get past the editor's desk have three main factors: a beginning that grabs, a middle that informs and uplifts, and a positive, conclusive ending. Following this pattern will give you the best chance of getting a manuscript published.

[Shirley] Take a look at articles you like to read. Study the way they're put together. See how an interesting, off-beat, or unexpected opening draws you in, making you hungry for more. Follow through the body of the story, which fits seamlessly with the opening and blends into the ending like melted chocolate, leaving you with a delicious aftertaste.

[Anne] Read several copies of magazines you hope to publish in. Note style, length, and topics covered. Your article must be a good fit, and it must be within their word count requirements. I once spent several weeks compiling a lengthy feature about the pros and cons of various movie genres, only to have it returned from a Salt Lake newspaper because I misread the required length—by many pages. What a waste of time. No matter how powerful the manuscript, if it doesn't comply with company rules, it won't be accepted.

A query letter can be useful. This is a proposal that outlines what you plan to write and how you plan to write it. Article queries and submission methods are different than for novels, which are discussed in a later chapter. The following information will help you compose a query that will make a magazine editor sit up and say, "Aha!"

First, make sure your target is accurate. Read several back issues of the magazine to check that your idea hasn't been covered recently. If it has, try to come up with a new angle for the topic—editors will often use a similar idea if the approach is different. Next, create an attention-grabbing opening sentence that will have the editor drooling for more information.

Your second paragraph can be bullet-pointed and should spell out what you plan to write with enough detail to be clear, yet concise. You don't want an editor scratching his head trying to read your mind. Believe me, he's too busy to bother and will toss your letter in the trash bin.

Follow your captivating inventory with a short paragraph that parades your knowledge of the subject matter and convinces the editor of your competence. If you have previous work to show, enclose photocopies of one or two of your articles. These are known as "clips." If this is your first attempt at writing articles, don't volunteer that fact. Let your writing ability speak for itself. Most query letters are best kept to one page, but if your topic involves in-depth research, then a second page of explanation is enlightening and acceptable.

One of the most vital ingredients of the perfect query letter is accuracy. Nothing shouts "amateur" more clearly than typos and misspelled howlers. Don't rely solely on your spell checker. Print out a copy, use a dictionary, and read with your brain in top gear—at least ten times—and with a night's sleep in between. When you and one other reader can see no faults, seal up your letter and send it on its way, along with a stamped, self-addressed envelope (SASE) for reply.

[Shirley] Sometimes you can tweak the same article to fit several different magazines, using the same subject, but approaching it from a different angle. For example, an article on how exercise can stimulate learning could work in magazines about the corporate world, women's health, or men's health. A parenting magazine could use the same article when focused on the benefits children can gain for a lifetime when good habits are established early. Naturally, you'll need to adjust article length to fit different editors' needs, keeping to the meat for shorter pieces, and filling it in with interesting anecdotes and quotes for longer features.

[Anne] The body of longer articles should include fascinating quotes. Use the active voice to make your story come alive. Your audience wants to feel involved, invigorated, and interested enough to finish.

Some years ago, a piece I wrote for an LDS Internet magazine came winging back with a note saying, "This is a great story, but please write it the way you write your novels. Make us feel the man's anguish, see his dilemma, understand why he acted the way he did, and let us know where he's heading next and why." I thought I had done these things, but on rereading my words, I realized it could be improved.

Ask yourself over and over, "Am I including answers to the questions asked by newspaper reporters?" (Where? When? What? Why? How? Who?)

Whenever possible, send pictures to enhance and clarify the feature. If an article is intended for a glossy color magazine, such as the *New Era* or *LDS Living*, I use 100 ASA slide film—and I take plenty of shots. This way, there is sure to be at least one good picture. Shoot close up, and try for natural-looking rather than posed photographs. Editors love to have plenty to choose from.

Publicity departments of some companies provide excellent pictures free of charge, as long as proper credit is given to the photographers. When writing an article for *LDS Living* about director Adam Aderegg and his movie *Charly*, I went to Excel Entertainment for photos of him. If you are writing for an Internet site and cannot find appropriate pictures, try a search on Google, where many resources are available. Remember, you must obtain permission to reproduce images, and you must give credit to the source. Often the person or people being interviewed will provide photographs.

[Shirley] There are some computer programs that let you edit an otherwise unusable photo. We had a family picture taken in our living room one Christmas that I wanted to post on my website, but there was so much clutter in the background that you could hardly see my family! My husband used Adobe Photoshop to cover the clutter with a soft, gray background. It brought our faces into focus and made our smiles shine.

[Anne] If interviewing is not your favorite thing to do, try writing down a checklist of useful questions. Be careful not to fall into the trap of topping the other person's remarks with some adventure of your own. If the focus turns to you instead of the person you're interviewing, the story can get lost, or take forever to emerge. Use questions that nudge and poke, ones that can't be answered with a simple "yes" or "no." And be ready to memorize any last-minute anecdotes or juicy statements that flow after your notepad and camera are packed away.

I used to take a small tape recorder to interviews, but this sometimes proved a deterrent to natural conversation and made me worry about changing tapes and loss of recording. I now use shorthand, making sure I translate to my computer as soon as I reach home. While memory is fresh, odd-looking scribbles can still be put back into real words.

In the past several years I have conducted several interviews by e-mail. I like this alternative for several reasons. The person being interviewed gets time to think about their responses. The material is more likely to be accurate. And e-mail lets you conduct interviews globally. If you choose celebrities for your subjects, most are flattered and willing to answer questions. Some are grateful for free publicity and might even send a copy of their book, CD, or whatever they produce.

Out of courtesy, I let interview participants know that I will be sending a draft copy, allowing them to reject anything they don't want published, and inviting further comment. I find interviewing is more relaxed this way, as people know the final printed version won't be twisted or misinterpreted. However, this method is not standard practice in the industry, because allowing the person to censor and edit can result in a one-sided observation of facts.

Personally, I feel comfortable doing interviews my way within the LDS community, but would choose the standard approach for any mainstream work.

[Shirley] When I interviewed people after the Manti tornado of September 2002, it was invaluable to have the interview subjects review the final story. Their completed individual stories were sent to them with a brief cover letter that stated a deadline for getting any corrections back to me. Like Anne, there were people who asked me to take some sections out, as they didn't want to risk potential embarrassment. There were others who clarified some points, and some who added to what was already there.

Unfortunately, there were a couple of people who missed the deadline. When they told me about it after the fact, I apologized. Then they said, "I know I didn't tell you soon enough." I was glad I'd given them a deadline for their feedback. The pie ended up on their face, not mine!

[Anne] If you cover general topics—such as exercise, weight loss, or nutrition—make sure it's something about which you are well informed, and preferably have experience with. True, there is an enormous amount of information on the Internet you could draw from, but nothing beats a true, personal yarn, from inside knowledge you possess firsthand.

[Shirley] If you're interested in writing about a subject, and know someone who has personal experience with it, you can work with them to write about it. You can even try it yourself—and you might even like it. Besides that, as a beginner, you could offer a fresh perspective as the new kid on the block. How does it feel to enter a gym for the first time, especially if you have a few bulges showing through your workout suit that aren't muscles? What is it like to take up calligraphy when your signature is an illegible scrawl? What is it like to be a parent for a day?

If there are subjects that you're interested in, but have no intention of experiencing, you can spend time doing research, and from that information, write a compelling and believable piece on anything—whether you've tried it or not.

Don't let anyone say you can't do it if you really want to. You can.

[Anne] One last thing about the nitty-gritty of article writing. Never send off a manuscript in haste. It is sickening to wish, too late, that you could edit further. Allow at least a day after your "final" rewrite for it to sit, then read yet again. Get someone else to do the same for you. Run a spell check, a grammar check, and a search-and-find for overused words like "the," "had," "also," "that," "too," "so," "really," and "very." See how many of these you can eliminate for tightness. It is surprising how much improvement you can make.

For example, I first typed that sentence in the preceding paragraph as: ". . . and a search-and-find for the overuse of the word 'the' . . ." I used "the" three times when once would do. When I removed my first "the" and rearranged the sentence, it felt less clumsy and better balanced.

One point to keep in mind is that despite your most creative and error-free work, freelance writing for the LDS magazine market is not as lucrative as the non-LDS market. The *New Era* pays a small amount (extra for quality pictures), as does *LDS Living*. With only twelve issues a year for the *New Era*, and six issues a year for *LDS Living*, and a world from which they can draw material, getting work accepted by these magazines can be slow and intermittent. But don't give up. Be like a newborn foal, keep trying until you're up and running.

[Linda W] You might also try writing for various regional LDS publications. I know of three in the west:

Desert Saints - a monthly magazine out of Las Vegas.
http://www.desertsaintsonline.com
The Arizona Beehive - a bimonthly newspaper with the LDS population as its target audience.
http://www.arizonabeehive.com
The Latter-day Messenger - an LDS newspaper that targets Northern California, Sacramento, and the Bay area.
http://chantaclair.com/ldm.htm

These are all paper-and-ink publications. The Arizona Beehive *pays 7¢ a word, and the editor likes pieces to be about 700 words, which comes to around $50 an article. This might not seem like much, but if you write two articles an issue, by the end of the year you will have made an extra $600.*

[Anne] Most LDS websites don't pay anything for articles, but it is still worth getting published this way because search engines pick up your name and add it to lists that people find when using search keywords. The more times your name appears on a search list, the more established your identity becomes in readers' eyes. Add a website of your own, and marketing takes on a new boost. Be sure to send your information to all search engines, and include a lengthy list of keywords in your appropriate metatag—a hidden page of codes behind all websites. This appears when you right-click on the page, then click on "view source" from the drop-down box.

For example, on my home page, the keyword metatag is:

> <meta name="keywords" content="LDS, movies, LDS movies, fiction, LDS news, news articles, Anne Bradshaw, Terracotta Summer, Chamomile Winter, Season of Fire, LDStorymakers, LDS publisher, Publishing Secrets, film, free, cinema, movie, family, values, screenplay, short stories, teenagers, youth, young adults, author, writing, novels, romance, intrigue, clean reading, clean books, Mormon, Christian, writer, publishing, books, reading, British Isles, England, Northern Ireland, Scotland, United Kingdom">

My metatag covers many variations that apply to my stories—words that people might use in a search when hunting down reading material.

Now for the promised submission help.

Most LDS websites contain a contact link. Sometimes this takes some careful scrolling and digging to discover, but keep looking—the link is lurking there somewhere. If it is not obvious, try a basic contact e-mail and ask for your query to be forwarded. Chances are you will be dealing with pleasant people and will eventually receive a reply from someone.

To submit an article for a glossy magazine, send it typed double-spaced, with no extra space between paragraphs. Indent the first line of each paragraph. Put your personal contact information (name, address, and phone number) in the top left corner, and the word count in the top right. Margins can range from 1 to 1½ inches.

Submit articles for websites according to the publication's instructions. Most sites don't require authors to add html, but if you find one asking for this, it is not difficult to learn the basics. There is an excellent site at **http://www.pageresource.com** that teaches html for beginners. For further information, try a Google search for "basic html" and choose from several options.

The following magazines, newspapers, and journals accept well-written articles and news stories:

1 - *Meridian* at:
http://www.meridianmagazine.com/
2 - *Mahonri* at:
http://www.mahonri.org/
3 - *Mormonchic* at:
http://www.mormonchic.com/
4 - *Desert Saints* at:
http://www.desertsaintsonline.com/
5 - *New Era*, send e-mail to:
cur-editorial-newera@ldschurch.org
6 - *The Friend,* send e-mail to:
cur-editorial-friend@ldschurch.org
7 - *The Ensign,* send e-mail to:
cur-editorial-ensign@ldschurch.org
8 - *LDS Living,* send e-mail to:
editor@ldsliving.com
9 - *Arizona Beehive*, learn more at:
http://www.arizonabeehive.com/
10 - *Irreantum*, Quarterly Journal of the Association for Mormon Letters (AML).
Send queries to:
Irreantum2@cs.com
11 - *Journal of Mormon History*, semi-annual journal of the Mormon History Association.
For information send e-mail to:
klarry@comcast.net

If you can see the benefits of article writing and can't wait to create, why not begin at once? Your only cost is time and a chunk of mental exercise. If your first story comes flying back or disappears into some editor's garbage, don't quit! Reread this chapter, do your homework, and type away until one day that welcome message arrives containing the breathtaking words: "We are pleased to inform you that your submission has been accepted."

chapter 4 Rub the Lamp, Make the Magic

SUBMITTING WITH STYLE

by Shirley Bahlmann

with contributions by
Lisa J. Peck & Linda Paulson Adams

So you finished writing your book? Great! There's nothing more fulfilling than getting a story that was running around in your head out on paper for people to read. You have a big advantage over the writers of even half a century ago. They were limited to typewriters and correction fluid. You most likely have the benefit of a word processor to help keep your thoughts in order.

[Lisa] Once the story is done, pat yourself on the back, and then get back to work—it's time to rewrite. In earlier days, precious few people had the dedication to write and rewrite the old-fashioned way. With the advent of word processors, more and more people are polishing manuscripts and submitting to publishers.

[Linda A] Ooooh, you have to love word processors. I can't imagine going back to a standard typewriter. Think about moving even one paragraph! It meant retyping reams of pages. And please, don't even think about not using a computer to type your manuscript. Editors will not attempt to read your handwriting.

Even if you're the next William Shakespeare, you have to type to even get in the game, and you will need an electronic copy of your work, as well.

[Shirley] Competition is fierce. Many national publishers no longer accept unsolicited manuscripts because they receive such a mountain of mail from unpublished authors. But take heart! There's always room for good writers who submit their best work. This chapter teaches you how to jump through the hoops that lead to publication. Not every would-be author will study up and do it right—but you're obviously not one of those, because you're reading this book.

REWRITES

After you type the final period, don't be too hasty in sending your work off to a publisher. Once you think it's done—that you've dotted every *I* and crossed every *T*—rewrite it one more time. Some authors feel rewriting "cramps their style," but with the competition out there, you can't afford not to. Some writers rewrite only once, some go through their story a dozen times. Usually certain sections of a book require more work than others. Do as much rewriting as necessary to smooth out those rough spots, but know that you probably won't have to re-write the whole book that many times.

Regardless of how you revise, changing your attitude toward revision may be the most important first step.

[Lisa] For some writers, rewriting is their favorite part of the writing process.

[Linda A] Not me. I enjoy the rush of energy when a story is first flowing. But I've learned that my rough draft stinks like the updraft from a landfill. And I never feel finished. I am constantly rewriting and tweaking and changing. It's so important. (Hey, can I change that last sentence, or is it too late?)

[Shirley] I actually enjoy rewriting. It's like walking down the path that has already been laid from the cottage to the castle. I don't need to wonder about where the road is taking me. When I rewrite, I get to walk the path again, trimming branches and planting flowers along the way.

[Lisa] Different styles of rewriting work for different authors. Some start at the beginning and go to the end, others go to specific places and "spot rewrite." However you do it, make sure that the final rewrite includes the whole book, start to finish.

[Shirley] One method many writers use is to let the manuscript sit for awhile—days, even weeks—before doing the final rewrite. Don't peek. Don't even open the file. This distances you from your work and lets you go back later with the objectivity you might not have had otherwise. For many writers it helps to work on something else during this time. Whether you start another story, paint your kitchen, or go on vacation, do it—so long as it has nothing to do with the book. This distance can help you see things that might get you rejected, things you wouldn't catch if you were in a hurry. Imagine wishing you could rewrite some part that isn't working, as your book sits unsold on store shelves.

FIRST READERS

At the end of your hiatus, pull out your manuscript and read it through with fresh eyes. Pretend you've never seen it before. Look for anything awkward and passages that pull you out of the story. Read your book out loud. For some reason, the spoken word is a great judge of how well the written word flows. Writers that do this always seem to find themselves rearranging words. This is a good way to weed out awkward phrases, avoid repetitive words, and ensure overall flow. It's especially effective for improving dialogue.

[Lisa] Even excellent wording can jolt a reader from your book if it stands out from the rest too much. Orson Scott Card once said

that whenever he'd find a passage in his manuscript that he thought particularly striking, he'd take it out. He'd rather the reader stay immersed in the book than notice his genius with words.

[Shirley] Mark the places you want to revise and keep on reading. It's best if you can do this in one sitting, or at least in large blocks of time. If you let too much time elapse between reading the sections, you may miss things that don't connect from the beginning of the story to the end. One of our authors realized she had a nine-day week in part of her story—the point being, you don't want to submit a book with obvious flaws. It isn't ready.

When you finish reading your entire manuscript, go back and fix the places you've marked. For many writers it is invaluable to have several people read over the manuscript with a critical eye. We call them . . . well . . . readers. They can find flaws you might never see.

[Lisa] They sometimes have great suggestions on how to make the story better. Plus it's priceless to get honest feedback on your work. It gives the writer an idea of how people respond to what's written.

Receiving feedback from readers and making improvements is vital to the final polish on a good manuscript. This requires tough skin. Realize that any time your readers mark something for you to consider revising, it's because they care about your success. Once you get their opinions, you can weigh them and decide if their advice works for the story. Never lose sight of the fact that this is your work, but give serious consideration to the things they say.

For example, in Hollywood, the ratings board (those in charge of rating movies) interprets one fan letter to represent 1000 people. For eight letters of complaint, they assume 8000 people feel the same way. It's wise to treat your proofreading this way. If two readers point out the same flaw, you can bet they won't be the only two people in the world to notice.

In return for their time, many authors give their readers a copy of the book and a mention in their acknowledgments. Professional readers can be hired, but most of us choose from friends and family.

Choose people who will be honest. When a reader reports that they loved everything, it doesn't do you a whole lot of good . . . except for your ego.

Many of us find it works best to give readers their own copy of the manuscript or a computer disk, allowing them to make comments as they go. Hard copies can take a lot of paper and ink, but in the long run it's worth it.

[Shirley] Once your readers return their copies, compile the feedback onto one manuscript, using a different color for each reader. With different colors you can see how many people made comments in specific places, and can better judge what must be changed.

Don't be afraid to cut things that aren't working. It never hurt a tree to get pruned. Roses bloom all season only if they're cut. You can—and will—improve your story by taking out things that block the flow, are unnecessary to the plot, or belabor a point.

A final word on rewriting is that you'll always find something you could change. You reach a point of diminishing returns when you are only changing a word or two here and there that don't affect the story.

When you reach the point where you'd rather just burn the manuscript than go through it again, you're probably done. At some point you have to stop and let the manuscript go. This is easier to do when you know you've taken the time to do it right.

SUBMITTING

You have the Great LDS Novel resting in your hard drive. Now what?

The next step is to find a listing of publishers and pick the ones that interest you most. LDS publishing houses usually list the type of books they focus on in their submission guidelines. Make sure you submit your book to one that accepts your genre, or it won't be published, no matter how good your work is. You can also find publishers listed in the *Writer's Market,* on the Internet, or in the phone book. Another method is to pick up books that catch your fancy and are similar to what you write, and see who published them. Contact information is generally listed in the front pages of any book. Send the publisher a letter or e-mail and ask for their submission guidelines.

National and LDS publishers are different in many ways. When looking for a national publisher, you usually work through an agent who assists you in getting your manuscript to the right people in the right publishing houses, negotiates your contract, and so forth.

[Linda A] This is similar to choosing a real estate agent to sell your house instead of selling it yourself. A literary agent charges a commission on your royalties (15% is typical), and for a first-time author it is next to impossible to break into the national market without one. However, LDS publishers do not work with agents. Acquiring an agent won't help you if you're trying to publish solely in the LDS market.

[Shirley] Each publishing house has its own submission guidelines. Some want to see your entire work up front. Others want to see just a query letter or sample chapters and a synopsis. Follow whatever guidelines the publisher gives you, and don't assume that what one house wants is what the rest of them will ask for. If editors see that you didn't take the time to study house guidelines, they often won't bother reading the manuscript, because it shows the author's lack of attention to detail.

Competition is fierce, and you want to make sure that you're not rejected just because you didn't have your page numbers in the right spot.

[Linda A] Actually—they probably won't reject you for a page number being on the left instead of the right, so don't have a panic attack if you realize after the fact that you mixed up a tiny detail; but they will *notice if you send a synopsis when they want a complete manuscript, or vice versa.*

[Lisa] An unsolicited manuscript is a manuscript the publisher didn't ask to see, and most publishers don't accept them. In the national market, as of this writing, Boyds Mills Press, Marshall Cavendish, and Atheneum Books are among the few that will. But since the publishing world is constantly changing, check Writer's Market *or some other reliable source to discover the current policy of any publisher you're interested in.*

If a publisher doesn't take unsolicited manuscripts, they may still look at a query letter and a synopsis of your work. The synopsis and query give an editor a feel for your book and help the house decide whether they want to see the whole thing. Your goal is to make sure that they do.

Even if a publishing house accepts unsolicited manuscripts, this path is often a very difficult one to tread. An agent can sometimes open doors that will see your book in print faster than if you tackle the national market yourself. On the other hand, often it's just as hard to get an agent who is willing to handle your manuscript as it is to find a publisher directly.

The LDS publishers that we have worked with all accept unsolicited manuscripts.

[Linda A] When an editor asks for the manuscript in response to your query, your book now becomes a solicited manuscript. When you send it, make sure to write "Requested Material" on the box or envelope, and remind them in your cover letter that they asked to see it.

QUERY LETTER

[Shirley] A query letter is a brief explanation of your book and an introduction of yourself to a publisher. In most cases, your query letter should not exceed one page in length. However, in *Renegade Writer* by Linda Formichelli and Diana Burrell, the authors state that on occasion they have sent a longer query with good effect. Remember, though, that these are experienced writers.

Keep in mind that you are writing a business letter, addressed to the managing editor. Include your name, address, phone number, and e-mail address (if any) so they know where to find you, should they want to see more. You may feel compelled to include a detailed outline of your journey from plot conception to book completion.

[Linda A] But don't.

[Shirley] To start, you need to capture the editor's attention with a sizzling opening line, perhaps a teaser for your book—something that piques their interest and pulls them into the body of the letter. Whatever you do, don't write:

> *Dear Publisher,*
> *I have written the best book you will receive all year. You ought to read it. You'll be glad you did and sorry if you don't. I'll send it "write" away. Ha, ha!*
> *With Love, N. O. Class*

Better something like:

> *Dear Publisher,*
> *When Joey steps outside one day, he's startled to find himself in a completely different world. The grass is blue, the pavement is polka dot, and even though the sun is rising, there's a smaller sun setting on the opposite horizon. Joey must determine what has happened and restore his world to its normal state before the day ends, or the entire planet will suffer a terrible fate.*
> *I published an article in the April 2002 issue of* Mind-Reader's Digest.
> *A synopsis of* Joey's Blue Day *is enclosed. Thank you for your consideration. I look forward to hearing from you.*
> *Sincerely, Iman Author*

The key is to get the editor's attention with a good hook, then show any past accomplishments. If they like your style and the concept, editors will likely request more.

[Linda A] Query letters are the bane of many authors. They can be as difficult as writing the actual book. Keep them short. Give a few compelling lines about your story, followed by brief information about yourself and why you believe this publisher would be interested in your book. Three short paragraphs can do it. There are whole books out there on writing good queries, and the rules are the same for either the national or the LDS market.

If you've published, say in the New Era *or* Irreantum, *or have educational or biographical credits pertinent to the work you're offering, say so. But don't pad your resume—letters to the editor of* The Daily Universe *or doing your ward newsletter don't count. You can be creative; for example, if your novel is about a Mormon mom of four, and that's what you happen to be, you can briefly include that. But don't go on to say that you were the editor of a prestigious unnamed newspaper when it was actually your PTA newsletter. If you don't have any real publications under your belt, leave that part out.*

SYNOPSIS

[Shirley] There are two types of synopses: one for authors and one for publishers.

An author's synopsis should include all the major plot points, contributing characters, and storylines. Some authors use the synopsis format as a pre-writing exercise so that they know where the story is going.

A publisher's synopsis is much shorter and focuses on the main conflict of your story. It can be as long as seven pages, but the shorter the better. It can take a long time and a lot of rewriting to get it right, but don't settle for less than perfect. To a publisher, a poorly written synopsis represents a poorly written book.

[Linda A] Sometimes publishers ask for outlines. This type of synopsis is still what they mean for fiction. One New York agent I worked with told me that agents, editors, and publishers are used to reading stories. Don't send in a traditional outline format, even if it's in complete sentences. I was lucky with Cornerstone when I sent them the wrong type of outline—which my publisher later told me "read like a soap opera, but the book itself doesn't." They were willing to look past that to the actual book. But other publishers may not be as gracious.

[Shirley] If you've written a complete manuscript, you have the ability to rewrite your piece to any specifications. Keep the style of synopsis in agreement with the style of your book—and keep it brief. For more help in writing a synopsis, you can find information on the Internet or in many how-to-write books.

SUBMISSION GUIDELINES

Once a publisher is interested in your manuscript (or if they accept unsolicited manuscripts), be sure to follow their guidelines for submission. If you don't play by their rules, they may shoot your manuscript straight back with a letter saying, "Thanks, but no thanks."

If the requirements are vague, or if you're not sure, below are some industry standards that would be a safe bet:

- Use at least one inch margins, double spaced, and printed on only one side. This is not the time for saving paper. You don't want your manuscript to look or feel cramped.
- Double-space the entire manuscript. Editors like to use white space for marking your manuscript, and this allows them that space.
- Print out your manuscript in a 12-point font. Choose a readable font, such as Times New Roman. Do not use fancy fonts or adjust the size or spacing in any way. Anything else (unless

specifically requested by a particular publisher) is unprofessional and gives editors one more reason to reject your manuscript.

In the old days, all publishers wanted manuscripts submitted in Courier font because editors could peg how many pages your book would amount to just by noting your page count. (Courier is a monospaced font, which means all the letters take up the same amount of space.) With the advent of word processors and simple word-count technology, this has ceased to be a concern. For several years, national books about writing have begun to reflect this change, recommending any easily readable font. Every LDS publisher that we're aware of will accept manuscripts in Times, and even prefer it (although they also accept Courier). Many top LDS authors have never used Courier to submit their work and say that their edited copies always come back for their approval in a Times-like font. If you're still in doubt about fonts, check with the specific publisher.

Another bad idea is to use fancy fonts in an effort to stand out from the crowd. You'll stand out, all right—as someone not to be taken seriously. Unusual fonts are not always easy to read, and an annoyed editor is not one you want making a decision about whether or not to publish your book. Your writing is the place to get creative, not your manuscript presentation.

- Put a header at the top that includes your last name and the title of the book. This information shows up on every page. Your manuscript will be loose, not stapled, and it could get dropped and scattered by accident. Wouldn't it be horrible for them not to know whose brilliant book that was, and not be able to contact you?
- Number the pages in the top right-hand corner. This can go in with your header.
- Use white paper only, no onion skin paper and no cardstock. Do not staple or bind the pages. You may use a large office-type clip if you can't stand it,

or a large rubber band, but it's not necessary. Some first-time authors think that if they send a manuscript on colored paper, it will make an impression on the editor, and perhaps be moved to the top of the stack. This tactic screams, "Amateur!" and is a fast route to the discard pile.

[Linda A] Oh, it makes an impression all right. The wrong kind! Also, never send chocolates or other gifts, for the same reason. Besides, chocolate can melt all over that nice white paper.

Send your book manuscript in a plain 10x13 envelope, or if it's too thick, send it in a sturdy mailing box. Magazine submissions of five pages or less may be folded into a standard business envelope. Don't decorate your package with stickers or markers. Leave it plain and professional. And do not write "Requested Material" on the outside unless it actually was.

You may include a stamped, self-addressed postcard that says, "We received your manuscript." When you get this back, you know your manuscript has been opened. The publisher might not send the postcard back, but it's worth a shot. Deseret Book is excellent at sending a postcard receipt to authors.

[Shirley] Also, resist the urge to gift-wrap your manuscript and tie on a ribbon. It might look pretty to you, but you'll look mighty desperate to the professionals in the industry.

- Include a Self-Addressed, Stamped Envelope (SASE), which allows the editor to return the manuscript if the house decides not to publish it. Assuming your manuscript returns in good shape, you can save the cost of printing by submitting the same copy to the next publisher.

[Linda A] The SASE is the single most important thing to include with your manuscript. Period. No SASE is the mark of a rank amateur. Publishers will not—repeat, will not—respond to authors that do not include the SASE. You may include postage

and an address label for the box, if you want the manuscript returned; or pack it in a box-within-a-box. You also have the option of saying, in your cover letter, "The manuscript pages may be recycled. Please use the enclosed SASE for your reply." Then you need only send a standard business envelope (#10) with your address and a single first-class stamp on it. You may want to figure out which costs more, the full return postage, or printing a new copy of the manuscript plus one stamp.

- Include a cover letter that tells a little about your book and a bit about you, why you wrote this, and how they can get in touch with you. This is like a query letter, still businesslike, but not as formal and is not meant to grab their attention. It's simply an introduction.
- The number of publishers who accept electronic submissions is growing constantly. If you can send a manuscript via the Internet, you'll save paper and postage. Use the same guidelines for putting your manuscript on paper, and e-mail it according to the publisher's specifications.

[Linda A] But do not e-mail an unsolicited manuscript to any publisher if you're not dead sure that they want to receive it electronically. Also check out which format the editor wants your e-manuscript to arrive in. Some may want a PDF file, some a Word document, others only text in the body of an e-mail, and so on. If you don't get it right, they may never read your manuscript. Due to the prolific nature of computer viruses, many editors are wary about the attachments they will or will not open, so you must follow their guidelines.

[Lisa] Give your prospective publisher three to six months to receive your manuscript and read it. If you haven't heard back in six months—and only then—you may send an e-mail or letter with a polite inquiry as to the status of your manuscript. Do not call! This is bad form and bothersome.

Don't just sit and watch the calendar pages fall to the floor while you wait. Get busy and work on another book. Keep those creative juices flowing.

Always have a plan "B," because it's possible your manuscript won't fit the publisher's needs. Have another publisher in mind to try, in the event that your book finds its way back to your door without a contract in tow.

Some publishing houses will accept simultaneous submissions. This means sending your manuscript to more than one publisher at the same time. If you do this, you must note in your cover letter that it is a simultaneous submission. You might cover more ground faster this way, but simultaneous submissions can work against you. If a publisher knows you sent your book to other houses, they might not bother even looking at it. For other publishers, knowing their competitors have the manuscript may actually speed their reply.

If the publisher states in their guidelines that they don't accept simultaneous submissions, don't send them.

Yet if you send it to one house at a time, and three houses take six months each to review it, you could spend years trying to get it published. It's up to you how you deal with this situation, but be honest and fair with the way you play the game.

[Linda A] You have to tell them what you're doing, or you may find yourself with more than one publisher wanting to accept your work. A happy dilemma, but unfair to all concerned. They need to know other people are looking at it, so they don't spend precious time developing marketing strategies, only to find out you have since gone elsewhere. Note whether a submission is or is not simultaneous in your cover letter. Also, if your work is accepted by one house, and you're ready to sign that contract, it's common courtesy to send out letters immediately to any other publishers who have your book to let them know.

After all, it's possible one of the others might want to offer you a sweeter deal. Whether that's likely or not, it's still fair game to let them know you won't need them this time—and that way you won't burn bridges.

A word on multiple submissions, which is not the same thing as a simultaneous submission. A multiple submission means that you sent the same publisher two or more manuscripts at the same time. Generally speaking, publishers don't care too much for this practice either, with the possible exception of things like picture books. This preference should be listed in their guidelines. Otherwise, send one house one work at a time, and wait until you receive a reply from them (acceptance or rejection) before sending another work to the same publisher.

REJECTED OR ACCEPTED

[Shirley] A refusal from a publisher does not mean that your manuscript is unworthy. Different publishers have different ideas of what they want to market. Even though you researched each publisher and submitted only to the ones that fit your genre, not every book fits at the time it is submitted. If the house you sent your romance novel to publishes ten romances a year, and they already have those ten for the year, you won't get fair consideration at that time. If any one of us who worked on this book gave up because we got rejected, we wouldn't be here today. It's hard to hear "no," but it's part of the process.

[Linda A] Bear in mind editors are only people. They might be having a bad day when they come to your piece. Or it doesn't fit their personal style. You have to try again and assume it wasn't the right fit. If a great pair of jeans doesn't fit the first person who tries them on, that doesn't make them lousy pants, right? The same goes for writing. It's so individual. Try someone else.

[Lisa] When you receive your rejected manuscript, send it on its merry way again, and keep on writing. Many authors make a game of collecting their rejection letters for when the book is finally in print. It's fun to read these with a smirk on your face.

[Linda A] Some authors burn them in the fireplace or flush them. I just keep mine in a file folder.

That brings me to another point. It's an excellent, brilliant, smashing, precocious idea to keep either a spreadsheet, notebook, or some other method to record where and when you sent out your manuscripts. If you have only one book, and you're sending it only one place at a time, chances are you're likely to remember where you sent it. However . . . imagine the utter embarrassment of sending the same book back to a place that already rejected it. Oops.

Plus, if you're like me, and have several short stories, poems, books, and query letters sent to multitudes of agents, magazines, and publishers at any one time, a tracking system becomes absolutely essential. It's a good habit. Plus, you might not forget where you sent your book, but you might forget how long ago you mailed it, and to whom, and wind up bothering them before it's proper. You can also track how long each publisher takes to respond, and note any trends.

[Shirley] I use a regular manila file folder for each of my books. I use the front of it to record in longhand when and to whom I submitted, and the date. If and when it comes back, I make another note of that date and move on to the next publisher on the list. It's old-fashioned, but it works for me!

[Linda A] You might get a rejection letter asking you to rewrite. Don't despair! This is actually very good news. The best thing to do then is rewrite—and send it back. Many, many authors have been published after an initial rejection. This means the editors were interested enough to give you commentary. Considering how busy these people are, that means you definitely got their attention with your story and writing skill. Any rejection letter with real ink on it is a good sign that you're getting close.

[Shirley] Another time to consider further rewriting is when a manuscript has been rejected multiple times from several houses. Listen closely to what the rejection letters say, if you are lucky enough to get back more than a form letter. Try to figure out what isn't working. Then rewrite and resubmit.

Of course this comes with the disclaimer that you own your artistic vision. Don't change what goes against your personal integrity for that work. But realize that if you've written a story no audience wants to buy, it could be excellent literature, but lacking marketability. You may have to sacrifice publishing that piece—for now. Keep trying with another work.

[Lisa] Now, let's say the publisher accepts your submission. You will likely get a phone call or a letter informing you of your acceptance and telling you the next step, which is often signing a contract. If this happens, celebrate! Then read over your contract carefully, making sure you understand each passage and are willing to abide by it before you sign on the dotted line. If you don't understand something, ask questions until you do. Some authors hire a lawyer to look over the contract before they sign.

[Linda A] If you want an attorney, make sure to seek out a literary contract attorney; someone who is familiar with ins and outs of the book-publishing world to help you explain what it all means.

This is where agents come in terribly useful in the national market, but note that this is not the major reason LDS publishers typically will not work with them, either. It has more to do with following the money.

Advances are up-front payments that authors may receive, based on royalties that the publisher expects you to earn. If you get an advance, you don't receive any more money until it's "earned out," or paid for by your sales, which can be a long time—possibly never, if the book flops. Agents make most of their income from a percentage of advances that they have landed for their clients.

LDS publishing houses rarely offer advances. They are comparatively small and just can't afford to take that additional up-front cost and risk. If they had to deal with literary agents hounding them for gigantic advances all the time, LDS publishers would quickly go out of business.

On the flip side, for most agents, the teeny tiny portion of that teeny tiny advance that they might be able to wheedle out of an LDS publisher is simply not enough to be worth their time, either. That's what the agent issue boils down to.

The major downside to authors not using agents is that we don't have a professional on our side to explain the contract before signing and to negotiate out any unpleasant or unfair clauses. Unfortunately, you should not expect a business deal to be sweet and perfectly fair and honest just because the people you happen to be working with are members of the Church.

Be wise. Contracts are always written to favor the publisher.

[Lisa] They will usually give you some time to consider and study the contract before you have to send it back. Don't take this opportunity for granted. Read it through, have people look it over, and make sure you understand the relationship you are getting into. Many an author signs while basking in the thrill of acceptance, only to find that they gave up royalties on certain printings, electronic copies, movie rights, etc. Some authors don't care about these things, but make sure you understand it and get your questions answered.

[Linda A] Always think about the "what ifs." If your book turns out to be a best seller, and they want to make dolls and action figures out of your characters, did you give up those rights? Maybe that won't happen. But it might.

I strongly recommend reading Writer's Market FAQs *by Peter Rubie. It's very helpful in explaining confusing contract clauses. Do your best to understand what you're signing, and remember there could be a small amount of room for negotiation before the publisher withdraws their offer and tells you to take a hike. If you are a first-time author, your clout and negotiating power is extremely limited, so use caution when requesting changes.*

(For additional information about contracts, see Chapter Eight, 'Til Death Do Us Part: Contracts.*)*

Still, I can't say strongly or often enough how important it is not to sign anything you're not comfortable with.

[Shirley] Now clear a space on your bookshelf for your upcoming book. Once you hit this point, it's time to plan your marketing and promotion strategy. Yes, you need to help if you're going to sell many books. While most publishers will do a certain amount of publicity, they can't really be expected to push every single book they print with the same fervor that the book's creator can muster. If the reading public doesn't know your book is out there, how can they be expected to buy it?

Read through Chapter Ten in this book titled, *Thinking Outside the Bookstore: Self Promotion.* After all, as the foremost authority of your book, who is better qualified to tell the world about it than you? (That is, besides your mother!)

chapter 5 You Think My Baby's Ugly?

DEALING WITH REJECTION

by Julie Wright

with contributions by
Josi Kilpack & Thom Duncan

Congratulations on completing your first book! Really, I mean that. Step one in getting published is to actually write the book, and it takes a lot of effort to sit a fanny in a chair and keep it there long enough to get to where you can legitimately type the words "the end."

[Josi] If I had a dollar for everyone who told me they want to write a book, they started a book, or even that they have a great idea for a book . . . well, I'd make more money with that than I make writing! You've done what most people never get around to doing, and you should glow with satisfaction.

[Julie] Once you decide it's time to publish this masterpiece, the very first thing you need to prepare for is rejection. Why? Because that's what it's all about! I'm not talking about the kind of rejection you get when involved in dating. That's a rejection in a genre by itself. I'm talking about the personal, "I hate everything about you, and your baby is ugly" sort of rejection. The kind that makes you say, "I stink; I'm a horrid writer. What in the world was I thinking when I submitted such lame drivel to an editor?"

Rejection makes us do crazy things: we cry, eat too much chocolate, shop, throw things, stomp our feet, gnash our teeth, get angry—or worse, despondent. So what makes it better? How does a person ever feel inspired to write another sentence again?

That's where our help can come in.

It took me years to finish my first novel. I started it relatively young when I lacked any real focus on getting it done. I knew I would finish when I finished, and it would immediately be a bestseller!

[Josi] She was fifteen when she started To Catch a Falling Star*! Fifteen! I didn't read whole books when I was fifteen. Amazing. And it* did *make her publisher's bestsellers list* and *was the best selling work of fiction for her publisher in the year 2001—she's much too modest. Sorry to interrupt—go ahead, Julie.*

[Julie] As I matured, I spent more and more time with my manuscript. I thought about it when I wasn't working on it and agonized over it when I was. It had truly become a *part* of me. Once it was completed, I remember staring at the computer screen of my laptop and bursting into tears in much the same way I did when they showed me my first child after giving birth. This novel felt as much a part of me as my own children, and I thought it was such a beautiful baby. I couldn't wait to show it off and have everyone else coo and tell me how beautiful they thought it was, too.

Step two in getting published is submitting the manuscript. Wanting to take the proper steps, I sent mine in to one publisher and waited. And waited . . . and waited . . . and after about six months I started to get very nervous. My "child" had been away too long. Was she okay? Did I leave something out of her suitcase? Did I make certain to pack enough socks and underwear—had I packed any underwear at all?

I had no idea she was going to be gone so long, and I wasn't sure what to do!

Then I received a package in the mail. It was a goldenrod, padded envelope of the large variety, and the oddest thing . . . it had my address written in *my* handwriting on the front. Weird! I wasn't worried really, just elated to have her home safe and sound—with a contract attached. I was certain about the contract. There was no doubt in my mind that they would love my baby as much as I loved it. I assumed that the publisher had used the self-addressed, stamped envelope because they were running a tight budget. I appreciated their thrift. They probably sent the manuscript back so I could cast it in bronze so as to always remember my humble beginnings! How thoughtful of them. Surely that was it.

When I went inside and opened it up, you can imagine my surprise to find, in place of the expected contract, a note—short and to the point. It said, in all caps and bolded print, "YOUR BABY IS UGLY!"

Okay . . . okay . . . it didn't say that *exactly*, but it essentially said the same thing. It was some polite version of, "We're very sorry, but currently this manuscript does not fit the needs of our company, and we thank you for submitting, blah, blah, blah."

It didn't say that exactly either; I'm paraphrasing. I'd give it to you exactly as they wrote it, but I no longer have the letter. (I'll get to *that* in a moment.)

I often wonder if it would have hurt less if the envelope hadn't been addressed in my own handwriting. It made the rejection that much more personal. They hadn't simply rejected the manuscript; they had rejected *me,* and in a sick and twisted way had involved me in the tragedy by using my own handwriting against me. They rejected the very fundamental part of me that created the person I was, and it was painful.

[Josi] My first rejection happened much the same way, except that I was dressed up since I had just come home from the temple. I saw the envelope and thought, "I'm being blessed for my worthiness!" There was no doubt in my naive little mind that this was my grand acceptance letter—maybe it was so thick because they had included a cash advance!

I click-clacked up the front steps in my heels and sat in a chair, taking a deep breath so as not to rush through such an amazing moment in my life. This was one of those moments I wanted to remember forever, one of those events I would one day tell my grandchildren about when they became discouraged with their own talents. I envisioned myself writing a book someday and sharing the experience . . . and . . . wait, here I am! Anyway, I ripped open the envelope and froze. Rejected! The letter said that my book did not fit into their schedule at that time.

I had to read the letter three times for it to sink in. Then I looked at the wall and started to cry. No one was home, and I just bawled. Imagine all the people I had told about the book! What would they think of me? It was a horrible moment that left me questioning everything. I put so much into that manuscript, and they had rejected it . . . just like that.

[Thom] For one whole year before I sold my first story to the Children's Friend, *I wrote a story a week and sent them off to various science fiction publishers. What I did to keep my spirits high during the near-constant rejection was to wallpaper my office with the rejection letters. It was great therapy.*

[Julie] As members of the human race, we should be used to rejection. From the days of picking teams for kick soccer on the playground, to dating, love, loans, job applications—anywhere the world can reject people, it does. So why does it hurt so much when it's a manuscript, and how do we deal with that hurt when it comes? And it *will* come. If you plan on publishing a book, you will experience the pain of rejection at some point.

[Thom] After all those rejections, the first novel I completed was published by the first publisher I sent it to. That was a new experience for me, having by that time accumulated over two hundred rejection slips for my short stories. Except for that story in the Children's Friend, *I had never had a story accepted the first time out. So, yes, you will experience pain, but if you stick with it—keep sending those stories or novels out—someday you will*

experience the supreme joy of some editor accepting something you've written and ultimately paying you money for it.

[Julie] In many ways, it's considered a rite of passage. Stephen King collected over 30 rejections for *Carrie*. The first Harry Potter book was reportedly rejected by 14 publishers (imagine their sorrow now—ouch!). So to be rejected is to be numbered with some of the best. If you get out of the fight without a few battle scars, did you really win? (Well, yes, but . . .)

Therapy is different for everyone. A lot of writers keep their rejection letters. I didn't save one. I'm a bridge burner that way. I sit in a dark room with sunglasses on and sob to music written to serenade depression. Then I get angry, take the rejection letter, rip it to shreds, and maybe stuff it in the garbage disposal. Or flush it, or burn it, or shred it, or . . . well, you get what I mean. Admittedly, pictures of ex-boyfriends met the same demise. It's satisfying to see the object of your pain swirling around the toilet bowl as it makes its way to the sewage system. Afterward, I turn off the depressing music, take off the sunglasses, and exit my cave to face the glare of the next day . . . and resubmit. That is my greatest therapy.

[Josi] I keep my rejection letters. I have a file for each book I've ever written. In it I keep research articles, statements, reviews, and so on. I keep the little postcard some publishers send when they receive your manuscript, and I save my rejection letters here, too. I find it to be kind of fun to go back and read a rejection for a book that just got a fabulous review—their loss!

From a healthier perspective, I've had some of my most valuable feedback in rejection letters. I mean, these editors read thousands of manuscripts every year, and if they say, "Your character wasn't fully developed," well, they probably have a point. Of course I rant and rave when I first read it, but a few weeks later, when my eyes aren't so swollen, I reread and often find very good information that helps me make my baby look a little better when I send her out to face the world again.

[Julie] Exactly. What Josi points out—and what many people fail to realize—is that a rejection can be a *good* thing. I remember going to a writers conference where the keynote speaker shared a story of a young actress rehearsing a scene for a play. She was on her knees, sobbing with real tears. She was so into her character that she was quite startled to realize the director was standing in front of her, tapping the toe of his wing tip shoe, staring down with a contemptuous scowl.

"What do you think you're doing?" he asked.

"I'm acting," she replied, wiping the back of her hand over her cheeks to dry the tears, her shoulders heaving as the sobs slowly subsided.

"Well, can you do it better?" he asked.

Better? BETTER*?*

Well . . . *can* you? Certainly you put your entire heart into your manuscript. You did the very best you could do *at that time*, but when you get a rejection in the mail, it's like that director tapping his toe, challenging you to do it *better.*

Read between the lines and see why they rejected it. Do you have a problem with too many adverbs? Is your dialogue missing that spark of realism? Maybe you didn't research your subject matter and need to hit the books longer to get it right. Maybe you have a great idea with a pretty good follow-through, but they can't take the time to cultivate you into the writer they see you have the potential to be.

[Josi] Check to see if they even read it! I've had manuscripts come back in a perfect stack, not one page out of place. That just doesn't happen if someone actually reads it. Sometimes the editors have too many books right then, or your cover letter was lame, or the front page had typos, and they assumed the rest of the book was the same. Look with a discerning eye and see if you can figure out any automatic reasons for the rejection.

The first time I submitted a manuscript I didn't put chapter numbers. I wrote CHAPTER but I didn't bother numbering them. Why, I don't know, I just didn't. I also forgot to do automatic page numbers, so I wrote them all in by hand, and had to scribble some out and such—but I didn't want to waste another half ream of paper! Surely they wouldn't mind. But they do mind—trust me. If they even sniff incompetence, you're toast. They have plenty of other manuscripts that follow submission guidelines to the letter. They won't waste their time with someone unwilling to do what it takes.

[Thom] I attended a science fiction convention once and heard a published author tell an interesting story that got me through those times of rejection. A manuscript that had been rejected a year before was accepted a year later by the very same editor who had rejected it the first time.

[Josi] I also know of writers who have resubmitted a book that was initially rejected—after revisions of course—and it was later accepted. So don't think that no means "NO WAY, not ever." But if you resubmit, make sure the manuscript is good enough to warrant their time to evaluate it again.

[Julie] Publishing has become a timid sort of business. Many publishing houses in the LDS market are apprehensive about printing anything they didn't absolutely fall in love with. Potential is tossed in the gutter on many occasions, due to the fact that publishers lack the means to make a writer into a best seller in our limited market, and the fact that they have a sea of manuscripts to choose from. A rejection should not be seen as, "you're not worth your weight in words," but as an opportunity to prove that you are. *Can you do it better?* Well . . . can you?

[Thom] Another way to look at rejections is that each rejection letter puts you one step closer to being accepted. I had a friend who sold insurance once and told me that if he made at least thirty cold calls during the day, he could get at least two appointments for that night. For every ten appointments, he sold half an insurance policy. The key was the thirty calls during the day. Fewer calls meant fewer appointments meant fewer sales. The same goes for rejections. The more you get, the sooner you'll get a sale. It's the law of averages.

[Julie] Once you get over your grief, all there is left to do is keep trying. Even in our niche LDS market, there is more than one basket in which to put your eggs. Keep trying. Try every available publishing house, and if they all refuse, make your book better and try again. Just as Thom said, the odds are in your favor if you keep submitting.

You could also consider joining a critique group. Let a fresh set of eyes look over your baby and see if they can make that piece of hair that sticks up in the back lie flat. Sometimes it means "killing your darlings." It is wise to be willing to cut out scenes—even your favorite ones—to aid the flow of the story.

With me, if my editor wanted a scene cut, it was inevitably my favorite. It didn't matter what the scene was; it was my favorite. In order for my manuscript to progress into a book with a lovely jacket sitting its little spine on a bookstore shelf, I had to be willing to kill my darlings. I had to be willing to let my baby go to the beauty parlor and get a makeover, so I wouldn't get the horrific letter in bold caps: "Your baby is UGLY!"

[Josi] This is never as easy as it sounds. You've put your essence into everything you wrote, but at some point you have to ask, "Is it worth keeping if it means only me and my mother will ever read a word?" If you can answer that with a bold "yes," then keep the troublesome scene, character, or symbolism, and be content with the realization that it might not ever be published. The fact is, when a reader picks up a book, they have expectations that must be met for the book to succeed.

Editors know this better than anyone. You might *not have to change your book, but you should be willing to nip and tuck it here and there if you want it in published form.*

You can't help but become emotionally attached to your book and your characters, but you can't afford to lose out on your potential because of something that can afford to go. My husband buys and sells a lot of real estate and such—he's truly gifted at it. One of his greatest strengths is that he's willing to walk away. No matter how much he may want something, or how much it calls to him, he will always walk away if it isn't working out.

[Thom] This may be easier said than done, but sometimes you should ignore what your critics say and write the scene anyway. If you really believe in the scene, or you really like the character, keep at it. Maybe the first publisher didn't like the scene, but maybe the second one will. Ultimately you have to be the one who decides what stays and what goes—don't be bullied into changes you feel strongly about. It is your book.

[Julie] Personalities make a strong difference in this situation. Like Josi and Thom said, what one publisher thinks is absurd, another will find witty and brilliant. Don't compromise your ideas for fame and glory if it's going to hurt you more in the end.

What if your first child never finds the light of the bookstore? Is that a good enough reason to stop trying? No! If you wrote one book, you can write two. There's no such thing as second child infertility in writing, unless *you* give up. While your first one is submitted, work on a second and a third. This not only keeps you from getting so connected to your first book that you can't let anything go, but it keeps new ideas coming and distracts you from obsessing. Keep reading, attending writers workshops, and writing. Make friends with other writers so you can share your disappointments and successes with them.

I found that sharing rejection letters with anyone (except other authors) gets you that pinched uncomfortable expression people get when your fly is down. No one wants to talk to you about fixing it, and they don't want to be around you until it's fixed, so they mumble some incoherent nonsense and slink away. Friends who are writers make it easier. They understand in ways the rest of the world can't, and they're not afraid to tell you to zip up your pants.

[Josi] Surrounding yourself with people who understand you is a real sanity saver. Of course you will have friends and family who "get it" and know what a vital part of you your writing really is, but look for others that really understand the processes. For me it has made all the difference in my writing and in my career—for one thing, my husband can tolerate just about as much writing talk

as I can tolerate first downs. It's sad but true, so save those who can't save themselves from you, and choose supporters who speak your language . . . or type in your font. You get the idea.

[Thom] Not only that, but other writers won't look at you as if you're insane. The non-writer, upon learning that you've been rejected dozens of times, will wonder what personality deficiency you have that keeps you setting yourself up for rejection. "Why don't you just quit?" they might say. Other writers won't say that. They will understand why you keep sending your stories out, even though you keep getting rejections.

[Julie] Regardless of the response you receive your first few tries at submitting, the point is to never give up on yourself. Live your dream so that when you get to the end of your life, you don't wonder what would have happened if you had just kept trying.

[Thom] This was very important for me. I'm fifty-five years old, and I remember telling myself back in my thirties that I didn't want to turn sixty not having at least tried to get published. I can walk into my seventh decade now without guilt, thanks to my telling myself what would have happened if I never even tried.

[Julie] After the rejection, the rewrites, and the growth they foster, there will come a day when a letter from a publishing house will arrive in your mailbox. I'm not talking about the *Clearing House* one with Ed McMahon on it. I'm talking about a thin envelope wrapped around an official-looking letterhead where the first typed words are: "I read your manuscript, and *loved* it."

[Thom] Or, in my case, you'll get a call on the phone directly from the publisher: "Brother Duncan, we want to publish your novel. I'll be sending you the contract and the galley sheets, which we need back in two weeks."

chapter 6

Inside the Chocolate Factory

Manuscript to Finished Book

by Linda Paulson Adams

with contributions by
Shirley Bahlmann & Lisa J. Peck

The moment of sheer panic hits about two seconds *after* you hand your precious manuscript to the post office employee and pay your hard-earned cash for the postage. It almost stops you in your tracks. *What have I done to my baby? Will they take care of it?*

Calm down. Don't sweat the nit-picky details of what happens at the post office. You can expect your package to be tossed around and possibly dropped, so make sure the package is sturdy. It's a terrific idea to get a tracking number on the package for your own peace of mind.

What is a remarkably *bad* idea is sending it Certified Mail or by any system that requires someone to personally sign for your package. They're busy people and might find this annoying enough that they'll even send your manuscript back unopened. If you use a tracking number, you can call or go online to find out where your package is, and know exactly when it arrives.

By the time you send off your manuscript, you will have already highlighted *Publishing Secrets*, checked off the key points with a red pen, and used the industry correct way to submit.

Now your baby is in the mail.

What happens if everything *works* and they want to publish your book?

Fear of success is a very real thing. I'll say this once: get over it, at least long enough to mail your manuscript. Success is good. Success is okay. But, yes, it can come armed with sweaty palms, anxiety attacks, and innumerable neuroses. Look at the statistics on how many movie stars wind up in drug rehab programs at the peak of their success, and you'll have to concede that there's something to that paradox called "fear of success." Be prepared. Have a plan for when that stress hits.

[Shirley] Hopefully, it's a plan that doesn't involve too much chocolate!

Linda's point is interesting. I recently spoke to a woman who has some incredible ideas for inventions that would make people's lives easier. She has wondered for over ten years why she never goes past the design stage. Even when she's seen a couple of her ideas produced independently by others and make a big splash in the retail market, she still sits and wonders why she's unwilling to take the next step. She wants to. She just doesn't. And she doesn't know why.

[Linda A] Take courage! It is not a crime to have great, even terrific things happen in your life.

[Shirley] Remember, man(kind) is that he might have joy! It says it right there in the scriptures. If you feel joy at the thought of sharing your God-given talents, then you're doing what you're supposed to. It may not be easy, but what, in a life that's richly lived, is?

I have a saying hanging on my wall that I believe with all my heart. "It's better to feel too much than too little." So feel the fear, if you must, and do it anyway!

[Linda A] In our happy acceptance scenario, your package arrives safely, is opened by an editor's assistant, and placed directly in a slush pile. Oh no! Slush? You said this was the HAPPY scenario! Hang on, it is.

It sounds horrible: your gem of a manuscript is stacked on top of that soggy brown mush that ends up on Utah curbs all winter long? No, not that kind of slush. The "slush pile" is where they put manuscripts they didn't ask to receive, that's all. Some of these piles get pretty huge. If you can imagine the laundry in my house with six kids under the age of fourteen when it gets backed up—well, that pile of eight thousand socks alone can't compare to some slush piles. But don't let that stop you. The editorial staff does get through it. Maybe even faster than I get through my laundry, because they have a *paying* job, and I, well . . . ahem. I digress.

Again, this is the procedure the LDS market follows. (Nationally, remember, you almost always must have an agent submit for you in order to land your synopsis on an editor's desk, not to mention an entire manuscript.) What this means is that you have a fraction of time to hook your editor's attention. They might not read every submission all the way through. They're not mean or evil; sheer logistics, or sometimes plain old poor writing, prevent them. But when this editor reaches *your* manuscript, she is amazed and intrigued. She just can't stop reading it. It's that good. Then she takes it to a committee meeting. It gets read and approved and usually goes on to a marketing committee, who figures out whether this story has sales potential.

Don't balk at this, either. Your book has to get a sales pitch. Publishers spend a ton of money producing each book, and cut you a personal paycheck to boot.

[Shirley] No matter how much your Aunt Lucy or Cousin John likes your story about Grandpa's dog Wiggles, your publisher has to determine the appeal of the subject for a wider audience. Who knows, Wiggles may become the next Old Yeller. It's up to the publisher and staff to determine if your book is one that will bring a return on their investment in time and money. If it seems they're taking a long time to answer, that's a good sign. It usually means they're seriously considering your work.

[Linda A] To publishers, great books are very much worth their investment. That's why publishers are in business. They spend money, but they also need to turn a profit. They love books, and they love discovering new talent and helping authors succeed.

So, during all the long months you sit at home writing your next masterpiece, your book is transported to all sorts of meetings and committees until, finally at long last, they agree: YES! We want this book.

[Shirley] I have to tell you from personal experience that the best cure for impatience is to pass the time writing another book. Pour that creative energy onto paper instead of using it to wear a path in your carpet as you wait to hear back from a prospective publisher.

[Linda A] No matter how excited they may be, they're still professionals. The acceptance letter or phone call will sound businesslike; the editor won't gush with undying praise.

If you get such a letter, it should include the words, "We are interested in publishing [name of book]." And a contract should be enclosed. Contracts. Oh boy.

Just reading the legal jargon can give you a headache. As excited as you are—and you should be!—doing your happy dance and calling every friend you ever knew, *don't* actually sign the thing until you've gone over it carefully, understand what rights you're giving the publisher, and what your obligations will be once everything is legal. This is as legally binding as the mortgage papers on your home. Remember that. As thrilled as you get over buying your own home, there's a lot you need to understand before you sign on that dotted line.

[Lisa] I wouldn't advise using a lawyer unless he or she has specific experience with book contracts. I've heard of many problems where a particular attorney didn't understand the book publishing world, with all the ins and outs with various rights. But do be sure to read the contract thoroughly and discuss it with those that do understand basic contracts and publishing. Do not sign what you don't understand.

[Shirley] If you have concerns over the contract, see if you can talk it over with your publisher. Have them explain sections that aren't clear to you.

[Linda A] And if they won't explain or try to sweet-talk you out of comprehension, that's not a good sign at all. Don't accept the phrase "this is normal for LDS publishing," or any such lines, until you've checked around and discovered that it really is.

[Shirley] Look into the possibility of talking over specific contract concerns with other published authors, as well. I have never signed with a publisher without talking to some of the authors who have already worked with that publisher—and the company should give you names of people you may contact, on request. Personal experience is an invaluable teacher. I make it a point to talk to more than one author, as each person's experience is different.

(For more specific information, see Chapter Eight, 'Til Death Do Us Part: Contracts.*)*

[Linda A] In this chapter, let's assume the contract is great, and everything is beautiful, with little additional negotiation needed. The downside is, your book won't be in print the month after signing. It can be twelve months to two years before you hold your book in your hands.

Oh, wait—when you signed that contract, you thought you were *done*? Ha, ha, ha . . . ha. You're hardly done *at all*, sweetheart. Ahead of you lies editing (several months), cover design (months), typesetting (weeks), proofing (weeks), and finally printing (months), and delivering to stores (another several weeks).

[Lisa] Plus if your book is going to be sold in Deseret Book stores, it must pass through the Deseret Book committee , which determines which books they will sell. It can take up to two months if you're a brand new author. But this won't even happen until after the book is released. It all adds up to lots of time.

[Linda A] Right. Thanks, Lisa.

I removed one or two potentially questionable sentences in *Prodigal Journey* before going to press, just to be certain it would make it through that Deseret Book process. If your book fails to receive that Deseret seal of approval, for whatever reason, your sales don't get out of the starting gate. It might not be the most attractive fact in the world, but that *is* the way things stand in LDS publishing. (Mentioned in more detail in Chapter One, *Honey, Take Out The Garbage: The Selective LDS Audience*)

Now. On to editing! This is where your book is turned over to editors to play with like so much modeling clay, and if you're not open-minded, it can make you scream.

Keep in mind that the editor's job is to make you look good. If you go into the process expecting a few bumps along the road, and you roll with it rather than fight every change, you'll be more pleasant to work with, and your editors won't get ulcers, either. They might even like to have you back for a second book, rather than dread ever working with you again.

[Shirley] What works best for me is to read the editorial comments and suggestions, and let them percolate in my brain for a day or two. Then, when I go back to the manuscript, I can see which suggestions strengthen the story or writing style, and which ones I'll need to talk to the editor about a compromise. If I were expected to sit down and decide right then what needed changing, I'd have a big, worried headache! Give yourself the time you need. Everything will fall into place if you follow your inner voice.

[Linda A] This is when your editors might say, "We don't like this character's name. Can you change it to—?" And it's some awful name you would *never* give your baby. Or, "This ending doesn't work. Change it." Or, "There are holes in the plot here and here and here . . ."

Stay flexible. Try to see their point of view. Most of the time they do know what they're doing, and the attitude of listening and being taught at the feet of the pros goes a long way. Then do the work they ask for. Change what you can afford to, even if it hurts.

Once in a while you have to stick to your guns. In those cases, present your arguments logically and without, say, screaming at anybody. Sometimes you win.

During the editing of *Prodigal Journey,* my editors wanted the main characters Peter and Alyssa to kiss on the last page. I fought against it. They insisted, and so I rewrote as directed. But I felt it was too soon for them, plus it didn't fit either character's personality. Before printing, we talked about it again, and my editor came to see that the kiss really didn't fit—thankfully! We removed the scene, and it now ends the way I intended.

[Shirley] In one of my pre-submission edits, I was told to take out a passage in Walker's Gold *where Mattie is at her grandfather's funeral, and her pantyhose starts to slip down. I considered it, and decided to leave it in. It fit her personality so well! Since the book came out, several people have told me that they love that part of the story. Sometimes the suggestion is just one person's opinion. Bottom line: you need to pick your battles in this industry.*

[Linda A] I lost some of my favorite sentences along the way. It's not exactly fun to be told your writing needs improvement. The sooner you get used to the fact that *yes,* it can always be improved, and editors are there to help you do exactly that, and they are *not* evil spawn from Pluto trying to destroy your universe, the better. Everything will go much smoother than if you dig in your heels and refuse to change one absolutely perfect word.

This may be perhaps the single biggest difference between successful authors and those who aren't. Nothing seals your doom faster than refusing to edit and revise.

Onward: editing is now complete. Once editor and author are happy, the manuscript goes to typesetting, book design, cover design, and formatting. This is where the *publisher*, not you, chooses what font the book appears in, how much space at the top of the page, where to put the page numbers, what the cover will look like, and all that itty bitty really annoying stuff—count your blessings that you don't have to worry about it. Also note that in many cases the author does not choose the final title, either. Just be prepared for that. I was able to keep *Prodigal Journey*, gratefully, but Cornerstone chose the series title *Thy Kingdom Come*, which was not among my top ten choices.

When that's done, you should receive what are called galleys. That doesn't mean a full-scale model of a ship's kitchen. It means an unbound copy of the typeset book, exactly as it will appear in print. If your contract doesn't mention galley proofs, you might not get them. That's something to think about.

I can't stress enough how vital it is to go over your galleys with a red pen and mark any typos or problems that you find. Have a proofreading party and invite your friends. If you don't catch it now, it's everlastingly too late. (Well, maybe not everlastingly. There's always that second print run to look forward to.) Typically, publishers send a hard copy by overnight courier.

I was on vacation when mine came through electronically for *Prodigal Journey*, and I missed a number of typos because I didn't print the pages out and catch them on paper.

Galleys are *not* the place to jump up and say, "Wait! I think Chapter 10 should come before Chapter 7, and I forgot to include this totally important scene, and my dialogue in Chapter 20 is all messed up, is it too late?" The answer is, YES it IS too late. All that should be done in *editing*. Galleys are for proofreading purposes *only*.

Why? Simple. Time is money. Fixing a handful of typos can be done at the last minute, which is why they bother to send you galleys to approve in the first place. The publisher doesn't want typos in your book any more than you do. But insisting on major edits at this point causes major time delays. These things should have been fixed earlier.

Mark any errors you find in the galley copy and send it back by the deadline they give you. Any delay on your part risks a later release date, or—worse—the publisher printing your book without your corrections.

[Shirley] I find it most helpful to read the galleys aloud. (This is also important to do before you even send it to the publisher.)

[Linda A] Then it's off to the presses. Most publishers do not maintain their own presses in-house. This means they negotiate a bid and a printing date with an outside printing company, and your book waits in line at the printer. It gets printed, cut, and bound according to the publisher's specifications.

Side-by-side with editing and final proofreading comes this creature named "cover design." You can't judge a book by its cover? Try not to. I dare you.

Contrary to popular belief, most authors do not design their covers, and have virtually no say in deciding what goes on them. It's nice if something in your contract gives you final approval for the cover. Chances are you won't get this, and if so, your baby could end up dressed in an outfit you absolutely hate. In the national market, authors rarely have any say in cover design, but some LDS publishers are more accommodating.

[Shirley] The same goes for titles. Your publisher may discuss this with you, but they ultimately decide what your book will be called.

[Lisa] Remember that each LDS publishing house operates differently. I have worked with several. Some let me have a say on who my artist would be on the cover, but that was about all the input permitted. One had two cover designs drawn up, and they picked the one I hated; "them's the breaks" of being a published author. Grin, bear it, and hope for better luck with the next book.

Other publishing houses I've worked with were more liberal on the author's input. I've been allowed to design my own. At other times I've made suggestions, such as telling them that the main character has brown hair, not blonde. Sometimes, I didn't see the cover at all until I was mailed the first copies of the book. If you are unwilling to have no input on the cover, consider that when deciding which house you're going to submit to and what's spelled out in your contract.

[Linda A] Only self-published authors have complete control over their own covers, and frankly, many of these hire a cover designer. If you don't have a degree in marketing or graphic design . . . well, let's just say authors aren't generally the best judges of what will actually sell.

[Shirley] For my first book, I wanted a rattlesnake poised and ready to strike. The designers did a mock-up, and I loved it. But everyone I showed it to said it put them off. The only reason they'd buy it would be because it had my name on it. One teenage girl said it looked like "Reptiles of Utah." The publisher took matters into their own hands and compromised, using a less-threatening snake skeleton and a wagon train to denote that the book was a collection of pioneer stories. Once it was over and done, I had to admit that their approach was much more reader-friendly.

[Linda A] Finally! The cover is attached to your masterpiece, the finished book is packed in boxes and sent to a warehouse, and within a few weeks, a box of author's copies arrives in the mail.

[Lisa] It typically takes a couple more weeks for the books to make it onto bookstore shelves. From that point, stores order your book as demand dictates. Deseret Book is famous for keeping a book on its shelves for six to nine months, as long as it's selling. But once a store sells out of a slow-moving title (about one copy a month), they rarely reorder. Other bookstores generally keep copies on their shelves for longer periods.

The first year is the important year, especially if it's one of your first books. That's the time to do signings, mailings to friends and family, speaking engagements if you can, and any other marketing.

[Shirley] There's nothing like going into a bookstore and seeing a book with your name on it sitting on the shelf. And it feels almost as great when people tell you, "Hey, I was in Deseret Book the other day, and I saw your book there!" You have arrived!

[Linda A] It's a wonderful feeling to hold your own *Real Book* in your hands for the very first time. There's nothing like it in the world.

To get there, believe in yourself and your goals, and don't give up. It's not so unrealistic. Really. And it's not silly or a waste of time or selfish or anything else all those people out there will try to tell you. It's like my mother told me when I was in junior high and came home crying, teased awfully for being so skinny. (Oh to relive that day *now* . . .) She said, "They're just jealous."

She was right. And now, I repeat: they're only jealous. Don't let them stand in the way of your dreams. Only the Lord can direct what path your dreams should or should not follow. The public has this remarkable talent for encouraging you to remain mediocre and generic, for saying that you'll never accomplish anything weird like becoming a published author, and therefore that it's pointless to try. Don't fall prey to that mindset. Keep telling yourself you *can* do it.

chapter 7 Full House or Royal Flush?

Subsidy vs. Non-Subsidy Publishing

by Tristi Pinkston

with contributions by
Shirley Bahlmann & Anne Bradshaw

When you begin the search for a publisher, you may find some falling into the category of "subsidy publishers." This means that the publisher asks the author to pay part of the printing fees, then pays that money back to the author over a period of time, based on sales. Several authors have taken this route. Others avoid it. What are the pitfalls and the benefits of dealing with such a company? Let's take a closer look.

When I searched for a publisher for my first book, I was offered a contract from a subsidy publisher. I was elated at the thought of being published, but *not* at the thought of paying money. I hadn't realized when I submitted the manuscript that a financial donation would be expected. My husband had been out of work for several months, and I couldn't afford to put up the money. It was quite the chunk of change, when we were watching every penny! I turned down the offer and kept looking, and two months later I landed a contract with a different company that handled the price of printing in its entirety.

In retrospect, I know this decision was the right one for me. As we've struggled to recover financially from that period of unemployment, I'm grateful that all the financial decisions and considerations were made by my publisher, and that I didn't have to find a way to pull together that much money. The sacrifice was too great, the gamble too risky. There are authors who have dealt successfully with subsidy publishing, and are pleased with the results. But taking that path was not what I needed to do to get my career going.

[Shirley] After several unsuccessful attempts at getting published nationally in the 1980s, I took up serious writing again in 2001, this time for the LDS market. I received yet another rejection before getting an offer—IF I would help pay part of the publishing costs. For our family, the price was steep: $2,900. After much discussion and prayer, my husband and I decided to take the chance. We secured a loan in order to get the book published. (Not the best idea in the world, by the way.)

Part of the publishing agreement stipulated that for every book sold over 2,000 copies within the first year, I would be repaid a dollar toward my subsidy amount. Once the year was up, the subsidy repayment would end.

That particular clause was a great motivator for me to get my book out into the public eye. Since I had written a collection of true pioneer stories, I was fearless in taking my book to shops, stores, and museums, any and every place that had anything to do with Utah history. If it hadn't been for the opportunity to earn our investment back within a specified time frame, I doubt I would have had the enthusiasm to spread the word so widely.

Not every place I went accepted my book, but enough did that I earned more than half of my subsidy payment back within a year's time. When the year was up, the sales of Against All Odds *totaled more than 3,700. I don't believe we would have reached that number without the monetary investment. We feel it was money well spent, since my subsequent books, which were published subsidy-free (at no cost to me), have been more successful than the first, and repeatedly earn spots on my publisher's bestseller list.*

My second book, Isn't That Odd? *sold over 1,700 copies in only two months, where it took the first book six months to reach the 2,000 sales mark. I can't help but think that the chance to recoup our investment generated intense motivation in me to advertise and sell my book, which paved the way for greater success with future books.*

[Tristi] Subsidy publishing can be a positive experience. Shirley achieved her success by going out there and introducing her book in person. She made it happen rather than sitting back and hoping that it would fall into place on its own.

[Anne] I'd like to add something here. Many people have a warped view of subsidy publishing. Some consider it the same as "vanity" publishing, and scorn and belittle authors for—in their view—not being good enough to justify traditional publishing. Choosing author participation is not the same thing as going the vanity route. Vanity publishing is where the author pays the entire costs of printing.

Since some authors self-publish because no one will accept their work, vanity publishing has earned a bad name. But an author's reasons for self-publishing are not always because they can't get accepted elsewhere. Some great writers have already published traditionally, but find many advantages, financial and otherwise, from being in control of the whole publishing process.

On the other hand, I've read some dreadful self-published books that are poorly written and will never sell enough copies to recover costs. Obtaining and believing a thorough, non-biased analysis from an honest reader who knows something about writing is invaluable. If the verdict is negative, listen and act accordingly. You will save a lot of time, money, and heartache. Use it as a prod to become more competent by studying the art and practicing until the next book is acceptable.

As a rule, publishers who ask for author participation, or subsidy, recognize that your book is well-written, but are not prepared to take the full risk of sponsoring a new author, in case sales don't meet the returns they need as a company. In other words, they want you to take part of the risk with them.

This is fair enough, especially when they publish your next book at no cost to you.

You will hear outraged comments like, "You've worked hard to write the book. You shouldn't be asked to pay. Money should always flow TO the author. They should be paying you!" That's all very well, but do they realize how hard it is to find a publisher ready to snap up new manuscripts? Reasons for rejection are not always because the novel isn't good enough. Sometimes the manuscript reader that day just wasn't doing a great job, felt unwell, or didn't like your style; the finance department says allotted money has run out for newcomers this year; or the pile of manuscripts is too high to keep reading.

If a professional editor has been over your book, you know it's a quality book, and you can afford to assist—then why not go for it? It is, after all, a step on the ladder. Your books will be in the shops, and your career as a writer has a chance to take wings. Plus, you will have learned a great deal about publishing in the process.

[Tristi] There are a couple of things to consider as you make your decision: Do you have the financial underpinnings you need to take this risk? If you sink this kind of money into your book, will you suffer in other ways? At the time the offer was made to me, the investment was impossible. Perhaps you have some savings, or could squirrel away extra money for a short time to cover the costs. Maybe you could take out a loan, like Shirley did. But if making this kind of investment would hurt you in some way, such as losing credibility among some readers, try another route. And if your books *don't* sell (heaven forbid), you could be making payments on that loan for a very long time.

Talk to publishers who don't require an up-front expense on your part. Shirley had great success with her book over the long haul, but if it's going to keep you from paying your bills and buying groceries today, seriously consider other alternatives.

Second, read the contract thoroughly and carefully to see what type of repayment they offer. Be aware of what the legal wording means, and know what you're getting into.

I have a friend who signed with a subsidy publisher. This writer has yet to see returns great enough to justify the original expense. Work out a plan, like Shirley did. Go out there, make your book known, and increase your chance of success.

Third, talk to the publisher about future submissions. Will they require money for books you publish with them in the future? Some subsidy publishers ask for money only on the first book. Once they see your sales are doing well, they take on the full cost of the printing for subsequent books—another good reason to get out there and get some publicity going!

Ask the publisher about their advertising plans, and fill in any gaps with your own efforts. Speak at libraries, book clubs, schools, Church functions, and any other venue that fits the theme of your book. Print up business cards with the name of your book to hand out. Get your name known!

The choice is really all up to you. Subsidy printing has its good points as well as the potentially bad. But if you go into it with your eyes open—aware of the pitfalls that may appear—you can prepare for every eventuality and not be taken by surprise.

chapter 8

'Til Death Do Us Part

CONTRACTS

by Julie Wright

with contributions by
BJ Rowley & Rachel Ann Nunes

As a novice writer, sending out manuscripts and query letters to publishers, your supreme hope is that any day you'll receive an envelope in the mail with a contract for you to sign. Most of us are starving for that contract—that irrefutable and tangible piece of legal evidence that will validate us to all the world as real, honest-to-goodness authors. And more importantly, to validate us to ourselves.

Here's the critical thing to remember and understand about contracts: they are the end result of a publisher's past experiences.

The items detailed in contracts are put there specifically to keep authors like you and me in line. More to the point, they want to keep us from running off to other presses. Publishing houses invest a significant amount of their time and money building a name for their authors and making them successful and profitable. They don't want you to take that hard-earned name away from them and make money for someone else.

It makes perfect sense to them. Nothing personal; it's just business.

But publishing contracts are written to protect publishers. They're not necessarily designed to protect you, the author. It's important to remember this when you enter into a contract negotiation, so that you are not there with the belief that it's all about *you.*

UNDERSTANDING YOUR CONTRACT

Generally speaking, if you publish in the national market, you will have an agent to look out for your best interests and balance the intricate details in the contract. Agents who have been in the business a long time know their way around and are excellent advocates.

In the LDS market, however, agents are presently scarce, and even frowned upon by many LDS publishers. This means you have no mechanism in place to protect your interests. You must be extremely vigilant and on guard.

This is not to say that the publishing houses in the LDS market are all tyrants looking to undermine your creativity and exploit your talent. Many definitely aren't. Just remember: they're looking out for *their* bottom lines.

The good news is: most author/publisher relationships *do* work to the satisfaction of both parties. It *can* be a win/win scenario.

So what are some of the things you should look for when signing a contract?

The first and best advice I can give you is this: take off those rose-colored glasses and keep your eyes open!

Writing books is not a Church calling. Neither is publishing them. Don't assume, just because this is the LDS market, that the publishers will all run their businesses based on Gospel standards and love. That would be a very naive approach. Business is business. Have some solid plans in mind for what you hope to achieve from your relationship with your publisher and what you want to see happen with the work being contracted. If you want your short story to eventually evolve into a book, or your book to be transformed into a screenplay for a movie, plan ahead. Those arrangements don't happen by accident.

In my own situation, I wrote an LDS romance novel. It was well received, and I was very pleased with it. Some time later, I had an opportunity to turn it into a screenplay and sell it to a production company. How exciting! My relief was prodigious. By some miracle, I had the foresight, while negotiating the contract for this particular book, to address this very scenario. I discussed with my publisher the possibility of movie rights and had asked them to spell out exactly what it would mean—for both them and me—if I were presented with the opportunity to market the movie rights. It all worked out.

On the downside, how many authors never even think about movie rights? Would you? Did I, when my first contract was slid under my nose? Nope. I signed first and read later.

Important! Don't sign anything that you don't *completely* understand.

This sounds absurd, I know. Would you really want to risk losing your first and maybe only chance to become a "real" author? Would you want to offend and insult the very hand that seems to be feeding you? What if they yank it away, rip it up, and retract their offer? You're sunk!

I'm not saying don't sign. I'm simply saying *understand* what you're signing. Take it to a lawyer specializing in publishing, if you have to, so he can read through all that legalese and translate it into plain English. That way you can make an informed decision and perhaps know what points you should try to negotiate.

[BJ] At the very least, talk with successful authors. Most will be more than willing to discuss contract issues and help you understand the fine print involved. Join e-mail lists and writers' groups, such as AML-List, LDSReaders, LDSWriters, LDSAuthors, WorLDSmiths, ANWAchat, and any others you find available. Attend seminars and conferences, and network with the sponsors and other participants. Exchange e-mail addresses, and begin to build friendships and form associations with others who are in the same boat—or better yet, who have already successfully paddled the canoe across the lake. You don't have to go it alone or jump in blind. There's always help available.

(Also see LDStorymakers contact information on page 194.)

[Rachel] If for some reason you decide not to sign a contract, this won't be your last and only chance. It really won't. If you have the talent and the drive, you will make it as an author. Another publisher will recognize the value in your work. I feel that it's better to avoid signing something you don't agree with or feel good about than to waste years writing under a prejudicial contract.

The good news is that, with very rare exceptions, publishers in the LDS market will terminate your contract if you insist. They may not like it, and the separation may not be pretty, but they will terminate. Of course, that's not the goal. The goal is to publish successfully and to be happy with your publisher, and vice versa. That's a real possibility, if you go into the relationship with your eyes wide open. Even if you do sign a contract that isn't all you hoped for, you must at least know what your exit options are.

[Julie] If you have questions about any part of your contract, you should either hire a literary attorney or talk to several LDS authors who are currently publishing in the marketplace. Yes, you can also call your publisher and ask them exactly what each section means. They should be more than happy to discuss the details of the contract. A WARNING here, however: Understand that the publisher will probably have a rehearsed response to each of your objections. Their goal is to get you to sign the contract with as few changes as possible. Other authors, or an attorney, will be more objective.

Keep in mind that by seeking the advice of an attorney, you may be more liable after you sign. You will be much less likely to win any argument that you signed under duress or ignorance. Regardless, it's up to you to understand the *implications* of what is written, not just the wording of each paragraph by itself.

The following is a list of some of the clauses that you can reasonably expect to find in your contract. Each deserves your close attention. Read everything thoroughly. Don't be ashamed to make requests for changes; it never hurts to ask. They may want it all, and you may want it all, but somewhere in the middle there's room for everyone to be satisfied.

RIGHTS

One of the first things mentioned in my contract was *rights.* Simply put, after I signed, they owned *all* of them. I owned none. It said: ". . . the sole and exclusive, entire, total, consummate and unlimited rights to the Work." *All* the rights. I didn't really grasp what that meant when I signed. I honestly don't even remember reading that part, yet it was the first line of my contract. I'm not upset—just annoyed with myself for being so unaware. I naively thought I could alter the book later and submit it to a national publisher for the opportunity to resell it in the national market.

But no. "All" really means *all.* The book is no longer mine. By signing the contract, I agreed to let go.

[BJ] Even then, you might still own the copyright. That's usually yours by virtue of the fact that you wrote what you wrote. But be careful. Even that *can be signed away, if you're not vigilant. If the publisher were to go out of business, or your book taken out-of-print, or your contract declared void for whatever reason, the publishing and other various rights will generally revert back to the original copyright holder. You definitely want to be that person.*

A lot of rights are involved here. The "grant of rights" clause in a publishing contract spells out the rights that are specifically "granted" by you to the publisher. They don't automatically acquire all those rights. You give them over.

Your grant could include all the exclusive rights and interests in your work—such as in Julie's first contract—which means that the publisher has total control over the exploitation of your work. Or the granting clause might be very limited and specific, such as only allowing the publisher to publish your work in a hardcover edition. Or it could be somewhere in between.

The main thing here is that the publisher can only exploit the rights that you grant them. Anything else is a violation of copyright law. The rights are yours to begin with—ALL of them—so it's only fair that you should have a say in which ones you sign over and which ones you keep.

For instance, why would you give away the movie rights to a publisher who has absolutely no potential of exploiting those rights themselves? And don't fall for the argument that a publisher might present that "because they published and publicized your book, they should *retain movie rights. After all, the movie offer would not have come along if they hadn't published your book." This is, of course, a bogus argument. A publisher should desire to publish a book strictly based on the inherent profit potential within their chosen medium—books, book-on-tape, etc. This is the* only *right they should retain.*

Other rights can include (but are not limited to) such things as: visual reproduction (movies), translations (foreign language or Braille), stage plays, audio reproduction (books on tape), electronic reproduction (e-books or CDs), foreign publishing, distribution, and even a clause for "future technology" or "derivative works." Make sure you read everything and cover everything.

[Rachel] If your book has national appeal, you may want to negotiate what happens to the rights if a national publisher becomes interested. Often the advance royalty from such a sale is split 50/50, but some authors may be able to put a cap on the amount they'd have to share. You also need to know what will happen to you and your contract if your publisher sells the company or goes out of business.

OUT-OF-PRINT CLAUSE

[Julie] Most contracts state that the rights to my book will return to me eventually, when and if the book goes out-of-print. But what does out-of-print really mean? Many times the terms and conditions of the phrase "out-of-print" are so vague that it can mean whatever the publisher wants it to mean. For instance, it might mean that if a publisher only sells one copy of your book in a 12-month period, they may be able to consider it still in-print and thus retain all the rights.

Find out what "out-of-print" means to *this* publisher. Ask them to spell it out in numbers and specifics, and to include this language in the contract. Is out-of-print less than a hundred copies left? None left? Some companies have been known to consider a book still in-print if they have a few dusty copies still sitting on a shelf somewhere in their warehouse. They might have printed that run two years ago, but because they still have a few copies left, they still own the rights.

[BJ] I know of another instance where books are still considered in-print if they're still being offered for sale in catalogs, websites, or even in retail stores—even though there might not be a single copy left in the warehouse at all. With the development of on-demand publishing, this has become a real issue.

[Rachel] One of my friends had a problem with his publisher where they had copies left, but the books weren't listed for sale anywhere. Basically, he was stuck unless he bought all the remaining copies himself. If he'd had the foresight to make sure that the out-of-print clause clearly stated that the books had to be available to retailers in catalogs, he could have taken the rights back much sooner.

Keep in mind that many publishers require a waiting period before rights will be returned, and sometimes they expect an author to write a letter requesting that the book be put back in print before they will officially return rights. Just like every other part of the contract, these items can be negotiated. Reprints can be a significant source of income in future years, so don't overlook this clause.

[Julie] Exactly. A vague out-of-print clause can be bad for you because it means the publisher can potentially hold onto the rights forever. Unless you specifically define out-of-print—such as less than X number of copies sold during the previous twelve months—this clause can come back to bite you in the backside, in either the LDS or the national market.

RIGHT OF FIRST REFUSAL (ROFR)

Most LDS contracts have an infamous "Right of First Refusal" clause that appears to permanently and perpetually seal you to your publisher—forever. (This clause is sometimes a paragraph on its own, or in a paragraph called the "Option Clause.") The ROFR means you are contractually bound to submit your next manuscript to that publisher first. In other words, they get first dibs on the next brilliant creation that springs forth from your word processor.

Okay, fine . . . Most brand-new authors don't really mind submitting their next book to their publisher. That's the whole point, right? Surely after that second book, you'll be a big enough name to go wherever you want anyway. Right?

But when you turn in that second book and are handed a new contract addendum to sign, guess what's in there? The Right of First Refusal . . . again! It's there every time.

I tried to eliminate this pesky little clause from one of my contracts. It didn't work very well, and I ended up relenting—due to my non-existent backbone in a confrontational situation! (I've wondered ever since what might have happened if I *had* stood up to them.)

I've been told that the best way to break a contract like this is to write something you know they *don't* want. They reject it, and you're off the hook. Sounds easy enough, right?

Resist this temptation. You can't expect others to play fair if you're not willing to play fair yourself. Besides, who wants to spend valuable writing time creating something of little or no value, or something you don't really want to write? And if you're in the middle of a great series, it might be difficult to take that series anywhere else except your first publisher, unless you get a superb lawyer and do fabulous battle in court. Remember, they wrote that contract clause to protect themselves, not you. They will very likely win such a battle.

[Rachel] This is where proper understanding of the ROFR comes into play. Notice that above Julie said, "This is the clause that appears to permanently and perpetually seal you to your publisher—forever and ever." Well, the truth is that it doesn't. Yes, you must allow your publisher to read your next manuscript and offer you a contract. But here's the clincher: you don't have

to sign. You are still free at that point to submit your baby to another publisher, and if you negotiate a contract that has better terms, you're free to sign and publish with that company instead. ("Better" being the operative word here—either financially or in regard to terms.)

[Julie] Keep in mind that your original publisher may have the right to counter-offer any other publisher's offer. If your contract has a clause stating that your publisher has the right to counter-offer, make certain it also states a time limit for them to make their decision. That way you don't hang eternally while the publisher drags their feet about accepting or declining your terms. It would be tragic to get stuck in literary limbo.

[Rachel] Interestingly enough, in talking with some of my nationally-published author friends, many no longer sign a ROFR clause at all. Rather, they sign a two- or three-book contract, receiving an advance for each manuscript as they turn it in. As long as they submit those manuscripts—often a series or a very specific genre—they are free to also publish elsewhere.

I have a contract like this with one of my publishers, and the respect I feel from this relationship makes me want to continue working with them. Other authors I know in the LDS market are also beginning to negotiate contracts with a ROFR that relates only to a particular series or genre. The market is beginning to make positive strides in this direction. But please don't feel that the ROFR (if it's only for your next book) is a negative thing in the LDS market, because in most cases this is something that works for both the publisher and the author. Publishers need to know that the author is planning to work with them for a few projects, and the author needs to know that their next book is wanted. Later on, when the relationship matures and your goals as a writer become more apparent, you can negotiate from there.

[Julie] In my situation, I made certain to specify that my LDS publishing house did not have first rights of refusal on my national or non-LDS work. I scratched out a sentence in the clause—after discussing it with them—and then reworded it right there in the margin before I signed. We both initialed the change. They didn't have to rewrite the contract, because the copy they received with my signature already had the necessary information. I was free to pursue my dream of publishing with a New York house for my non-LDS fantasy series.

[Rachel] Some LDS publishers may give you the right to sell your national work elsewhere, but may want to retain the right to exclusively distribute your national work in the LDS market. I know one author whose national agent had a real problem with this because national publishers already have their outlets and didn't want to have to negotiate with a smaller company for distribution. You might want to consider separating national and LDS work completely.

[Julie] You can also try restricting the ROFR by word count, genre, style, pseudonym, etc.

ETERNAL RIGHTS

As members of the LDS Church, we hold fast to the idea of eternal relationships. But eternity is for you and your family—not your publisher. There has been a great deal of concern in the LDS literary scene about the existence of an LDS book contract claiming that you must forever and eternally submit ALL future works to that publisher, as opposed to only your next book. Authors should be leery of this type of contract.

[Rachel] You, of course, would never sign a contract for a fast-food restaurant job that makes you covenant to work for them for the rest of your life. You wouldn't even consider this if it were a well-paying executive job. The idea is ridiculous. But, hey, this is publishing. You'd cut off your right arm to publish if you had to, right? (Well, maybe not, since you'll need that arm to write more books . . . but you get the point.) So when you talk to the publisher and they refuse to budge, you may feel that you

have no choice but to sign. Or maybe you didn't understand what you signed at the time you were offered the contract, and now you feel you need some breathing room.

Is everything lost? No.

An acquaintance of mine, a local, reputable attorney who has worked with authors and publishers in the LDS industry, writes,

> *Although the law is not crystal-clear on the subject, "contracts for life" are unenforceable. This would be for several legal reasons.*
>
> *First, every Utah contract must be supported by sufficient consideration, and there is no consideration a publisher could give to support such a contract.*
>
> *Second, such a contract would violate Utah public policy, and be an "adhesion" contract, and thus not enforceable.*
>
> *Lastly, I think a court could well construe such a contract term to be the result of duress or a sort of blackmail, and thus unenforceable. If such a provision were taken to court, the provision would fall.*
>
> *I doubt that any publisher would ever want it tested in court, preferring instead to maintain the intimidation/discouraging effect that it obviously has on writers, both new and experienced.*

In our research for this book, we found many LDS authors who once signed an eternal ROFR contract and who also eventually parted ways with their publisher. But we couldn't find any authors who had been taken to court by a publisher trying to enforce this clause. This seems to indicate that if the authors make a firm stand and negotiate, they will be freed from the contract or given terms they feel more comfortable with. If this becomes a concern for you, we recommend doing your own research and checking with legal counsel. ***The only person responsible for whether or not you sign a contract is you, the author.***

Under this eternal ROFR contract, you do have the right—at least on paper—to take a rejected manuscript elsewhere.

Unfortunately, another problem may arise if you do. Most LDS publishers do not care what you do with a manuscript they have rejected. In fact they wish you well in placing it with another company. Yet authors with the eternal ROFR contract report receiving a letter from their publisher basically saying that if they publish the rejected manuscript elsewhere in the LDS market, their future with them (their current publisher) could be in jeopardy. This means that if the author wants to continue publishing with that company, they must accept this solitary opinion that their work has no value in the market and shelve it indefinitely. All the long months of work and creativity are wasted. The irony is that several of my most successful books—ones that have garnered the most sales, literary acclaim, and positive fan mail—were ones initially rejected by a publisher (one actually being published in the end by the same company that had originally rejected it).

Even if authors still choose to submit rejected manuscripts elsewhere in the LDS market, they won't be able to offer their next book to that new publisher because of the ROFR with the first company, thus decreasing their chance of acceptance at all, since a publisher generally won't jump at publishing a single book from an author.

Taking all this into perspective, the biggest problem I see in such a contract is the uneasy relationship that it creates between the author and the publisher—a relationship based on coercion and fear rather than mutual respect and trust (which trust is very possible in this market, I promise). However, most new authors are so anxious to publish that they are willing to sign anything. And no one who has been in their place can blame them. In fact, I remember feeling exactly the same way!

[BJ] So do I! Yet if all authors refused such unhealthy contracts, the few publishers who have them might rethink their strategies. The idea is to create a positive working relationship—one beneficial to both parties. It's a give-and-take situation—or at least it should be. Publishers who consistently treat their authors well will have authors who are loyal.

ROYALTIES

[Julie] Another area that requires your close attention is how your publisher intends to compensate you for your work. What is the royalty percentage? Is it fair and competitive in the current market? Is it based on the retail price of the book or on the wholesale price?

And what *is* the wholesale price? Is it affected by promotions and giveaways? How often are they going to pay this royalty? Once a month? Twice a year? What about returned books?

While there is no "standard" royalty as such, there is a general range that you can expect from LDS publishers.

Royalties for hardback books might fall in the range of 8% to 15% of retail, with softcover royalties falling between 6% and 12%. Some publishers' royalties are built on a graduated scale. For instance, softcopy royalties might start at 6% for the first 5,000 copies, then grow to 8% for the next 5,000, and 10% thereafter. Hardbound might pay 8% for the first 5,000, 10% for the second 5,000, and 12% thereafter. Other publishers might pay as much as 10%, 12%, and 15% respectively for hardbound books.

Graduated royalties take into account the fact that the first run of your book—especially as a first-time author—represents a greater risk and cost to the publisher. As books sell, and print quantities increase, both the risk and the cost per book are reduced. Additional print runs generally are less expensive than first printings, since the layout, formatting, and editing have already been done. Once publishers are comfortable with their return on investment, they will be more willing to pay higher royalties to the author.

Established authors often do not have a graduated royalty clause, but begin right at the top.

[Rachel] Look closely at any small clauses. For instance, you might find one specifying that books sold at a promotional price will result in a smaller royalty. Or sometimes a publisher may state that for a certain period of time you will receive a lower

royalty. Since LDS publishers—especially larger ones—sell most of your books in the first three months after publication, this is important to know. Ask for specifics. A very small clause—a tiny sentence—can cut your royalty potential in half.

The standard response from publishers is that the extra money they receive from a promotional clause is to promote the author. However, it should be noted that an author's royalty is generally designed from the outset to allow a certain amount of promotion—without any promotional clause whatsoever. When most LDS authors do the math, they discover that the amount they sacrificed after signing a promotional clause usually does not equal the amount the publisher spent on promotions (unless, perhaps, your book sells very small amounts—in which case it would have been given only the basic promotions that are done for each and every book as a matter of course).

One author I know was horrified to discover that because of the promotional clause in her contact, she lost over ninety thousand dollars in potential royalty! Very few—if any—books in the LDS market get that much spent on their promotion.

When you do receive your royalty statement, be sure that you understand it. Double-check it against your contract.

For several years, until the bugs were worked out of a new royalty program at one publisher I worked with, I found simple accounting errors in my statements—one of which totaled over five thousand dollars! The errors weren't intentional, but had I not caught it, it's likely the amount would never have been adjusted.

Publishers are usually glad to explain how royalties work. I've called on the phone, scheduled meetings, and been impressed with their willingness to decipher royalty statements. Other authors who publish with your same publisher can also be a good resource. So if you have questions, the best thing to do is to start asking.

(For more information about Royalties, see Chapter Eleven, *Writing as a Legitimate Career*.)

LARGE RETAILER ROYALTY CLAUSE

[BJ] Another clause to be aware of is the "Large Retailer Royalty Clause" (often referred to as the Wal-Mart clause, "rack jobber" clause, or another similar name). This states that if a single, large vendor (such as Wal-Mart, Costco, Seagull Book, or Deseret Book) were to place an order for over 5,000 books at one time, then the author would get royalties on those books based on the publisher's net (or wholesale) rather than the retail price of the book.

The wholesale discount to a vendor of that size can be anywhere from a few dimes to a dollar or more. Either way, author royalties per book are slashed to approximately one-third to one-half of what he would have earned normally. The publisher's profits from the sale, however, usually remain the same, and are sometimes even slightly higher because of the smaller amount they're paying out in royalties.

Still, that doesn't sound so bad—at first glance. Better to make a few pennies on a LOT of books, than more pennies on not-so-many books. Who wouldn't want to see a few 5,000-book orders placed?

But hold the phone.

A problem arises when chain stores buy the larger number of books specifically to get the lower price, and then return them in large quantities later. This actually means that an author could end up owing the publisher back a significant portion of the money he was given in the first place. This happened to a friend of mine. He sold less than 3,000 books when all the returns were in. The bottom line? Well, his publisher ended up making more money (paying out less royalty and selling more books), the retailer made money (buying books for less, even though they didn't end up selling the whole 5,000), and the consumer saved money (buying the books on sale). The only one to lose in this situation was the author, who wrote the book, and on whose dream everyone profited. He really wondered if all the work had been worth the very small amount he had earned. If his publisher had sold smaller quantities at the regular wholesale, he would have received a lot *more in royalties.*

[Rachel] I've also had several friends in that same position, and though they sold more books than your friend, they were

disappointed. The question remains: Is a large retailer clause really necessary in such a small marketplace where there are few stores who can even buy that many books?

I know a successful LDS author who simply ***refused*** *to sign a contract with this clause. As a result, his book was not carried in Wal-Mart or some of the other general-market retail outlets. However, he determined that in the end he sold just as many books as he had with previous books. His fans found his novel in traditional LDS bookstores, and he made no significant sacrifice in royalty income.*

With one of my publishers, I negotiated my percentage off of the wholesale or net price (larger than my usual percentage off the retail), which means that if they do sell at a discount, my only penalty is my percentage of their reduction. They eat the rest. I feel this really limits huge discounting, keeping the value of my books up where they should be.

It is interesting to note that some LDS publishers have now eliminated or significantly reduced their sales to Wal-Mart and Barns & Noble. What affect this may have on the market is still to be determined. Also, some of the publishers who do sell to Wal-Mart do not make their authors sign a large retailer clause.

EDITING

[Julie] Often a contract will spell out editing procedures, and understanding these rights is particularly important. Some actually allow a publisher to change a manuscript without an author's approval—anywhere from a paragraph to a total rewrite! Most authors would not be comfortable agreeing to such a clause. Be sure that you have a say in what changes are made in your book. Remember, it's your name on the cover, and you will be held accountable for anything inside. You will also want the right to review the final typeset or galley copies.

[Rachel] Most publishers are really good when it comes to this. They want to keep the author happy and build trust. They know that the more eyes on the manuscript, the cleaner it will be.

They are only too happy to allow the author multiple chances at editing and proofreading. Occasionally, you will find an editor who, because of time deadlines, other pressures, or simply because of personal arrogance, does not follow this procedure. I know several authors who had short manuscripts accepted by a reputable publisher. They were never allowed to see the edited manuscript, and when they received their published books, each found a glaring error that they were sure they would have caught, had they been given this courtesy.

Years ago, a similar thing happened to me on a very short piece. Though it was in my contract that I would be able to see it before going to press, the editor went ahead without my approval, and to this day two tiny additions—not errors, really, but definitely not something I would have agreed to add—haunt me to the point where I almost hate that version of the story.

Don't be discouraged by these examples! I know it all sounds involved and confusing, but these things can all be dealt with satisfactorily. I've worked with many good and conscientious editors over the years—editors who respect my work and my writing style. I recommend discussing editing procedures with the editor before signing your contract. I like to go through my books once after they're edited, then again after typesetting. Editors are wonderful, but they don't catch everything (neither do writers!). In fact if you find a book with fewer than ten errors in the first printing, you have a well-edited book.

(For more information on working with editors, see Chapter Six, *Manuscript to Finished Book*.)

COPIES OF YOUR BOOK

[Rachel] It is customary for a publisher to give the author free copies of their book after they're published. The number of these books in the LDS Market ranges from ten to thirty copies, and the amount is almost always negotiable. Most publishers will let you buy additional copies of the book at or below wholesale. At wholesale, you may receive royalties on those same copies, while at below wholesale you won't. This will be outlined in your

contract. Some publishers encourage you to buy and sell as many books as possible, while others specifically state that your personal copies are not for resale.

TIME LIMITS

[Rachel] Time limits are an important consideration in your contract. As Julie mentioned above, not having time limits regarding certain aspects of your manuscript could leave you in literary limbo far longer than you should be. Several of the most important time limits are: how long a publisher has to accept or reject your manuscript, how many months they have to publish the book, and how long it must be out-of-print before the rights revert back to you. If any advances are involved, the timing for payment should also be addressed (very few advances are offered in the LDS market). Some publishers may spell these out for you as a matter of course, while others are more reluctant. Also, you may assign other time limits on just about any right you have granted.

NEGOTIATION

[Julie] Remember that you have the right to negotiate any part of your contract. I've personally never seen a contract that requires you to accept an offer all or nothing. (That doesn't mean publishers won't try to get you to sign without negotiating.) You should have the right to refuse or renegotiate a contract handed to you for a subsequent work.

[BJ] Most publishers do have a "boiler plate" contract that they offer to all new authors. A few publishers will absolutely refuse to change them, but most have no problem scratching out a few lines and initialing it, in order to keep their authors happy. If a publisher refuses to make even minor changes, this may be your first hint that perhaps you might be better off seeking another publisher who will be more willing to meet your individual needs.

Regardless, after you gain some years of experience and a strong fan base, you will have the clout to negotiate. Even many established authors don't realize that they do have this power—that they can and should *negotiate. In fact, doing so will actually help newer authors rising in the ranks. Their example could be pivotal as this market grows and matures.*

THE LDS MARKET

[Julie] Most of the other clauses in a publishing contract are fairly self-explanatory with a careful reading. But one last thing to remember about the LDS market is the way the market itself works. Certain bigger publishing companies have their own retail outlets and bookstore chains, and they have their own agenda as to how things should be done. Again, it's nothing personal; it's just business, and everyone is looking out for their own bottom line.

Why should you care if publishing companies own their own stores? Simply put, if you're being published by a smaller press, you need to be concerned about your book appearing in those major stores.

Things to consider: Does your publisher have a rapport or affiliation with the big chains? Will they be effective in placing your book in their stores so that you can get maximum exposure to the larger public?

[Rachel] This is a very important aspect of LDS publishing that I didn't understand before publishing my first novel. I knew that Deseret Book the publisher owned the chain of Deseret Book retail stores—the name connection was obvious—but I wasn't aware that the president of Covenant Communications also owned Seagull Book.

Currently, these two retail chains (Deseret Book and Seagull) represent about a third of the LDS marketplace each, with the remaining one-third share going collectively to the independent stores. Now that I understand this fact, it makes sense that Deseret Book will feature Deseret Book titles in their stores, that

Seagull will feature predominantly Covenant titles, and that the independent stores may actually carry more variety from all LDS publishers, large and small.

In this publisher/retailer connection, the LDS market is very unlike the national one, where large publishers legally can not own large distributors or retail chains. It will be interesting to see if this aspect of the LDS market changes in the future, as it has in the larger Christian market, where publishers have sold off their stores.

A FINAL WORD

[Julie] The good news is that you've been offered a contract! You've learned enough that someone wants to publish your book! Congratulations! Once you feel comfortable with the details of their offer, by all means proceed, sign your contract, and grin with worthy satisfaction when the validation as an author arrives in the form of a bound version of your creation, complete with *your* name on the book jacket.

[BJ] And after successfully wending your way through all this legal mumbo-jumbo, you earned it!

chapter 9

Fine, I'll Do It Myself!

A Look at Self-Publishing

by BJ Rowley

with contributions by
Rachel Ann Nunes & Marsha Ward

All right, either the chapter on contract headaches threw you completely off your groove, or you did your research, properly submitted your expertly written, carefully formatted manuscript to every LDS publisher known on planet Earth, and now you're sitting there holding an equal number of "Sorry Charlie" letters in your hand.

Nobody wants your masterpiece. (Gasp!)

They've given you every excuse imaginable: it's not their area of interest, the wrong genre, bad timing, they can only do so many books per year, yada, yada, yada. But deep down inside, you know—you just *know*—that your work has appeal and is a valuable and marketable commodity. After all, every single one of your preview readers loved it, and they're already clamoring for the sequel.

But what can you do?

Well, you can either dig out your most recent edition of *Writer's Market* and start querying national agents and publishers (not such a bad idea), or throw your hands in the air like I did, and proclaim to the four walls of your little writing cubicle, "Okay, fine! Be that way. I'll just do it myself!"

[Rachel] I remember thinking just that. But let me add a word of caution here. Hopefully, amidst all those rejection letters, there aren't too many telling you what a poor job you've done of writing and editing, or that your story makes no sense. Those aren't good rejections, and most likely mean that you need to develop your story further. However, if editors have said they really enjoyed your book, were impressed with the writing, and so forth, that is a fairly good indication that self-publishing might be a viable option for you.

[BJ] Good point.

[Marsha] I'm sitting here thinking, "I've so been there, done that!" My own background in publishing is as a journalist for LDS newspapers, where I have amassed a huge amount of credits and very nice kudos on my writing abilities. But my first love has always been fiction. When I submitted my novels, I got a lot of "negative marketing reports"—aka rejections—in my chosen national market. I knew I wrote tight, well-crafted, clean novels, but since they were set in the American West during the 19th Century, the window of publishing opportunity was limited to a few New York houses. They simply couldn't take on an unproven author and fit her books into their limited and highly formulaic lines.

My primary objective in self-publishing was to prove that people would buy what I had to sell. I chose not to open a new publishing business, but to get the help of a "hybrid," or as one company calls itself, a "digital publishing infrastructure provider." More on this later.

[BJ] My path to self-publishing was a bit different than most, in that I originally had two books published by a major LDS publisher before suddenly finding myself out-of-print due to circumstances beyond my control. I eventually corrected those situations, but by then my previous publisher and I had parted ways, leaving me out in the cold with two out-of-print, yet modestly successful books on my hands, and a third as yet unpublished sequel—not to mention all the stories still rattling around in my brain, yearning for release.

[Rachel] My path was also somewhat unusual. At the time, I had eight best-selling books in the LDS market with one of the larger LDS publishers—and several more scheduled for release. They didn't want this particular book because it didn't fit into the romance mold that they *had created for me. Another top LDS publisher told me it was well-written, and they loved the story, but they didn't know where it could fit in their plans. When a national agent tried to pitch it to her agency for a movie deal, I knew that if I couldn't find a publisher, I would have to do it myself. I had a very strong impression that I needed to get that book to my readers. I think to self-publish successfully, you must feel very strongly about it.*

[BJ] After being shut down in the LDS arena, I pursued the national market unsuccessfully for almost a year before finally determining that the LDS market was where I really wanted to be—and was intended to be—at least for the immediate future. But what could I do?

At about that point, I had occasion to discuss my options with Orson Scott Card, who happened to be in my ward at the time. His initial response came as a surprise. He told me, in no uncertain terms, that in order to be self-published, I would have to make significant and costly sacrifices to my writing. Publishing is demanding, he told me, and requires a level of dedication to the business and other aspects of the endeavor, which, he claimed, would detract significantly from my time and ability to create successful writing. In other words, it's almost impossible to be a great author and a great publisher at the same time.

I thought long and hard about what he said before it finally occurred to me that, in all likelihood, Scott just didn't enjoy the publishing end of the process. He's a writer—and a darn good one. Taking off the writer's hat to become an editor, designer, and business manager was perhaps not something he took pleasure in doing. Fortunately (for all of us Card fans), he didn't have to.

[Rachel] Scott was right. Self-publishing does take a lot of work if you want to be successful. It also takes a lot of time away from your writing. But there is something infinitely satisfying in having done it all yourself, similar to the satisfaction you feel the first time you accomplish any hard task. Plus, you learn a great deal about the whole publishing arena along the way.

[BJ] After more deep thought, it also occurred to me that I *do* enjoy the publishing aspects of the process—almost as much as the writing. I like designing my own covers, doing my own typesetting, editing my own books, and even taking care of the nitty-gritty business details. In fact, I'm pretty good at all of it—if I do say so myself.

In the end, I took the plunge . . . and have never regretted it for a minute.

[Rachel] I agree, BJ. I would think very hard about doing it again, but I have never regretted it.

[Marsha] Nor I. I'm having the time of my life.

[BJ] The bottom line is that self-publishing *is* a valid and legitimate option—one used successfully by many authors, both LDS and otherwise—whether you've been unilaterally rejected or not. It's also the only option that does *not* involve contracting with another individual or company for release of any publishing rights. You keep it all and give nothing up. That may attract some writers, in and of itself.

But self-publishing is not without its pitfalls and perils.

In this chapter we'll present some of the basic advantages and disadvantages of taking the do-it-yourself route to publishing. After we discuss the pros and cons, if you decide it's something you want to pursue—and more importantly, something that you would enjoy doing and could do well—then we'll provide a basic rundown of the steps involved in producing an LDS-marketable book on your own, and turning a profit in the process.

THE PROS AND CONS

RETURN

There's no question about it. The profit margin is bigger when you're the publisher of your own book. The less fingers in the pie, the more pie you get to keep for yourself. That, in and of itself, is a mighty powerful incentive to self-publish. Why let someone else make all that money, when you could pocket it yourself?

The industry standard for royalties is about 7¢ on the dollar of the cover price. That doesn't sound like a big return for a product selling to the public in the neighborhood of $15 each. The problem is all those fingers! Everybody wants a piece of your delicious pie.

First, the publisher sells books to bookstores and retailers at a substantial discount from the suggested or printed retail price of the book—typically 40%. That leaves the wholesale price. There's not much you can do about that, self-published or not. Publishers live in the wholesale world.

From that wholesale chunk of the pie, the next big slice gone is the cost of printing and binding. Very few publishers do their own printing (in fact, none in the LDS market at this time that I'm aware of). Publishers shop around extensively for the most competitive press bids, and will sometimes have books produced out of the country to bring those costs down. If you self-publish, you must locate those competitive printers, collect bids, and pay the price for the printer (unless you happen to have a four-color offset web press in your basement). This is a fairly constant expense, and one of the most determining factors involved in the financial decision-making process.

After printing, what's left of the pie is sliced up and divided out between book and cover design, typesetting and layout, editing and proofreading, legal requirements, shipping and warehousing, and business overhead (salaries, operational expenses, and so on).

Almost as an afterthought are those pesky author's royalties. No wonder your slice is so thin by then. Naturally the publishers need a few crumbs left over for themselves, when all is said and done. That's how they stay in business.

It's a fine line publishers tread to keep the price of the book reasonable and affordable, while managing to retain a profit after giving away so much of that pie.

The obvious advantage, if you are both publisher and author, is you get profits *and* royalties rolled into one. More pie for you!

[Rachel] We'll talk more about this when we address marketing, but I want to make an important note. It is true that you can earn more with self-publishing, but only *if you sell enough books. I was fortunate enough to have an established readership, which made self-publishing more successful in the long run; my self-published book ended up earning more than any of my other books, except one. But it was also a lot more work and time—time I could have used to write an entire new novel. Since writing is my real love, I continued with established publishers rather than self-publishing additional books. Each author must decide what's best for his or her situation, but it is possible to make self-publishing a very successful venture.*

CONTROL

[BJ] Another compelling reason to self-publish is to have total control over the finished product. *You* determine the final outcome. On the other hand, with a publisher you are at their mercy for many elements of your book. Even though you created the masterpiece, many times you don't even get to decide the title, let alone design the cover. Additionally, editors and proofreaders will change punctuation, grammar, wording, and occasionally require significant changes in content, to meet their standards and expectations. The first thing I was asked to do with my very first book was to rewrite and eliminate at least 10,000 words. They didn't want to risk so many pages on a first-time author.

Doing it yourself, you won't have to worry about what the design department dreams up. Every element of the book is yours to command. You create the title. You design the cover. You write the backliner. You have the final say about the entire content of your story—what stays in, what goes out, and how many pages it turns out to be. You control the proofreading and cleanup of the finished manuscript. You even decide what fonts to use, how to lay out the chapter headings, where to put the author biography and acknowledgments.

And—best of all—you get to put your own name on the title page, as big as you want!

When you're done, it will truly be your book.

[Rachel] This is probably the most attractive aspect about self-publishing. You are the ultimate editor. You decide each word to include or delete. I've worked with about eight editors over the years, and while some are really good, there are a few—usually young and inexperienced editors a year or so out of college—who basically try to fix things that need no fixing. One of my editors changed "he threw a kiss" to "he blew a kiss." I don't know about you, but these are two very different things in my mind. Besides, such a change was unnecessary. One author I know was irritated when an editor kept adding "wet" to a sentence describing a woman's hair, when the woman's hair wasn't supposed to be wet! Sometimes it's enough to drive you mad.

In self-publishing, you can simply turn down a suggestion, if you don't want it. It's very freeing—exhilarating, even.

[BJ] On the other hand, to be fair, there's a lot to be said for the old cliché "two heads are better than one." Most publishers have professional editors and proofreaders on staff or under contract who may see legitimate problems that you don't.

Publishers also have experience in marketing and selling books, and typically have a pretty good feel for what works and what doesn't when it comes to cover designs and titles and even the size of the book.

MARKETING

This may be the single biggest, yet least understood, hurdle for a self-published author. While it may be immensely satisfying to sell dozens of books yourself to all your family, friends, and acquaintances, unless you have a *lot* more of them than I do (and I have over one hundred first cousins), you're not going to break even on your own. In order to be profitable and successful, two things have to happen:

1 - You have to sell your books to retailers.
2 - Retailers have to sell your books to consumers. The more the merrier.

The established publishers definitely have the home-court advantage with the retailers. The larger publishers have their own chains of retail outlets, which cater to their own products. They are reluctant to carry books from other publishers, even well-established ones, unless they are proven titles or authors that will guarantee profitable returns. Taking on products from a self-published (especially first-time) author can be a great risk to them.

Independent bookstores know who the established publishers are and have gained confidence in their products. Most of these store are also reluctant to take on products from self-published, self-distributed authors. For one thing, they don't have the assurance that your book has met the LDS market standards and will be acceptable to their patrons. They generally won't have the time (or interest) to do their own content review.

Additionally, they will be reluctant to add you as yet another source for buying products. Bookstores want to streamline—to be able to buy from the fewest possible sources, to maximize their buying power, shipping, and time constraints. Shelf space is also at a premium, and the managers want to put books in that space that will turn them a profit. They just don't have room for everything.

The best way to overcome the retail obstacle is to contract the services of a distributor. Retailers know that self-published products coming through an established LDS distributor will already be approved for content and standards, giving them that needed level of confidence in your product.

The bookstores and retailers are already buying products from these same distributors, so your book does not add significantly to their overall process. Your book is automatically included in the distributor's product list.

Another advantage to using an established distributor is that they will handle the complete order-taking and shipping process, and possibly the warehousing of your books.

[Rachel] Some distributors are also able to get you into local stores of national chains, such as Media Play, Barnes and Noble, and B. Dalton. If you combine this type of distribution with book signings, you can sell significantly more books.

[BJ] Obviously there's a price to pay for this kind of service—another finger back in the pie. Distributors deduct a percentage of the sale to cover their services—typically around 25% of wholesale. But without a distributor, marketing to retailers is almost a lost cause. Not impossible, but very costly in terms of time, effort, and end results.

[Rachel] Research distributors before choosing one. The best way to do this is to contact LDS stores directly and ask them what they like about each distributor, and which is the easiest to work with.

[BJ] In order to overcome the second obstacle—marketing to the consumer—you almost certainly will have to pay for some advertising. And that means more money out of your pocket. As Anne pointed out in Chapter Three, just having your books on the store shelf won't guarantee that patrons will find them, or want to buy them if they do. You need your books and your name to become known to the LDS public, so that people will come looking for them.

To accomplish that, you'll have to fork over some real, hard cash for ads in such places as Books & Things, Deseret Book Club, Seagull Book & Tape, and other such catalogs. Radio, newspaper, and TV ads are also an option, although potentially expensive.

[Rachel] I have to say that any book I've ever seen go really big, whether self-published or otherwise, has a marketing plan that includes TV and radio ads. The truth is that most people watch a lot of TV and spend a lot of time with their car radios on.

An established author I know who is self-publishing has allotted $16,000 just for marketing, hoping to sell at least 20,000 books. (Remember, I said this is an established author. Most self-published people are doing great if they sell 3,000 to 5,000 books.)

Another successful self-published author spent over a million dollars pushing his book. Fortunately for him, the investment paid off, and he eventually signed a profitable national contract.

Most of us have much smaller budgets and must work to find creative ways to achieve additional exposure. The important thing is to do the research before you set down your cash. Talk to marketing people and successful self-published authors, and discover what they did. Read books on self-promotion. You will find many ways of getting the desired results.

[BJ] Free advertising, such as press releases and book signings, are always to your advantage, but require a certain amount of effort, preparation, and legwork to bring about.

[Rachel] You're right, there are many ways to get free advertising. One that I've had some success with is contacting newspapers and pitching an interesting angle on my book, so they will do an article. Book signings, speeches, and appearances are also helpful. But like BJ says, it takes a lot of legwork (with the emphasis on work*).*

You won't have a publicist setting up appointments and interviews for you, unless you have the money to pay for one. Every step in the marketing process takes time away from your writing and your family. You need to find the balance that works for you.

[BJ] So the big question is this: after going to all the trouble, time, and expense of producing your book, can you successfully market and sell it? If not, you better have plenty of room set aside in your basement for permanent warehousing. The bottom line to self-publishing, as Rachel mentioned earlier, is that, while you may enjoy having more of the pie to yourself, there is a distinct possibility that your hoped-for ten-inch deep dish might be closer to a mini-tart. In retrospect, 70¢ per book on thousands of books might be more appealing than three or four dollars per book on only a few hundred.

TO BE OR NOT TO BE

If you've been rejected across the board, the nicest advantage to self-publishing is that you are, in fact, published. You can legitimately and officially cross the line from being a "writer" to being a "published author." For many, there may be no other way to break in.

[Marsha] Since breaking in was definitely my goal, I'll tell you how I did it.

I investigated and rejected the idea of solely self-publishing. It wasn't right for me, so I checked out an alternative: what some people loosely term "POD Publishing." I say loosely, because it's a misnomer. The print-on-demand companies I looked into offer the services of digitizing your text, designing a cover, providing an International Standard Book Number (ISBN), registering with distributors such as Ingram and/or Baker & Taylor so your book will appear on Amazon.com and other online booksellers, and linking up with the actual POD printer. They have a complete line of optional author services, too, such as editing and providing marketing materials.

Many traditional publishers use the technology of POD or print-on-demand publishing for short print runs or test marketing. That's exactly what I needed to do: test market my novels.

I knew self-publishing wasn't going to be a forever situation for me, so I did my homework on the Internet and investigated companies that provide a complete printed book (or electronic book) along with some marketing avenues. Xlibris and 1stBooks are two such providers. Also among the pay-for-digital-setup companies are PageFreePublishing, VirtualBookWorm, and Booklocker. Some of these companies began with publishing electronic versions of books, or e-books, then began to offer print books as well. Others began as POD providers. I chose one of the latter, iUniverse.com.

For an affordable fee, I sent my first novel, complete with backliner and short review blurb, to iUniverse. I also provided a photographic image to incorporate into the cover design. About four weeks later, after I had the opportunity to proof the company's work twice, my book was available for sale!

Since then I have hand-sold a respectable number of books, given talks to library groups, reaped rave comments from readers and reviewers, and seen a thoroughly satisfying response to my efforts. Now I am a published author, and have used the same company to bring out a second novel. I proved my point—my novels are marketable.

DOING IT YOURSELF

[BJ] As I mentioned above, the two main components of self-publishing are *production* and *marketing*. First you produce the book, then you sell it. Following are the steps involved in the production process and some recommended methods for accomplishing each task. Marketing, advertising, promoting, and selling strategies for your self-published book are basically the same as if you publish with a regular publisher. The major difference is that as your own publisher, you foot the bill and take all the risk.

(I won't be touching on the marketing aspects here. See Chapter Ten, *Thinking Outside the Bookstore: Self-Promotion*.)

Let's assume you already did the principal writing and are now at the point where you either submitted, or would be submitting a manuscript to a publisher. It doesn't make much difference in the production process whether it's fiction on nonfiction. Most of the steps are the same. However, statistics do show that nonfiction self-published books have higher sales records than fiction.

Now you take off the writer's hat and become a publisher.

PRODUCTION PROCESS

EDITING

This part comes easiest to most writers. In fact, some authors are proficient enough at editing that their publishers have very little left to do with a submitted manuscript. If you're not accustomed to editing, then I recommend that you find family, friends, or acquaintances who have these skills. Many of these people will be more than willing to help, in return for a free book and a mention in your acknowledgments.

The first step is to do a thorough *content* edit of the book. This involves looking for storyline problems, inconsistencies, wording changes, loose ends, point-of-view violations, characterization, problem resolutions, LDS standards issues, etc. For nonfiction it also involves checking facts for accuracy.

The second step is the *line edit*. This is where grammatical problems are addressed and corrected.

The third step is to do a final and thorough *proofreading*, where any lingering typographical errors are picked up and corrected, and punctuation problems—such as misplaced commas—are fixed.

[Rachel] I'm sure BJ will agree with me when I add, please, please, whatever you do, don't do all the editing yourself! No matter how proficient you are, some things will inevitably escape your notice. And you will never, ever make a book successful if it's full of errors. For beginners, I suggest a minimum of three content editors. Two could be your writer friends, the third a professional editor. Give them clean copies of the manuscript, and when they return them, make whatever changes you agree with.

Then use another three line editors with three new copies of the manuscript to catch anything the first three might have missed. It's okay to use one or two of the previous editors to line edit because they'll be familiar with the story and more likely to catch additional errors. After you've made all the changes, go over it yourself at least two more times to be sure there are as few errors as possible. Yes, it's time-consuming, but editing is something on which you should not skimp if you self-publish.

When errors are found in the published book (as they will be, no matter how careful you are), you won't have anyone to blame but yourself. As I've said before, fewer than ten errors in a published book means it's been well-edited.

TYPESETTING

[BJ] Once the manuscript is rewritten, corrected, and polished to near perfection, you're ready to move on to the typesetting phase. This is where your word processing document is converted into a press-ready format (what used to be referred to as camera-ready). When you're done typesetting, what you see on the screen is exactly what the book will look like when printed.

Printing companies all have their own specific requirements concerning the file types and formats that they will accept. Be sure to check with your printer for their exact specifications. Two of the more commonly accepted formats are QuarkXpress and PageMaker. Some POD (Print On Demand) printers may prefer the files in PDF format. These professional software packages are not cheap, but older versions are often available on eBay and other online auction sources.

The typesetting can be contracted out. But if you want to retain total control, you may want to do this yourself. Typesetting software is fairly intuitive and user-friendly, but it does require practice and patience to obtain the desired results.

Before beginning your own typesetting, you'll want to peruse LDS books already in print—particularly those similar to your own—and determine just how you want to your book to look. Different publishers use different fonts and layouts. Find one that suits your tastes and needs, and duplicate it in your own typesetting layout.

In addition to laying out your manuscript, use the typesetting software to add in all those extra pages, such as the title page, copyright information, acknowledgments, author biography, and for nonfiction books, the bibliography, index, and so on. Again, the best advice I can give is to study similar published books and find the layout and arrangement that works best for you. (If you use something extremely weird or different, it may be hard to read and unappealing, and therefore will not generate much in sales.)

Once typesetting is completed, copy your typeset file, plus all fonts and images used, onto a CD or ZipDisk for the printer. And back up your file!

As a point of reference, all of my self-published books were typeset using QuarkXpress. I used Agaramond for the interior text, font size 12.5, with a line spacing of 14. Margins were set at ¾" all around, with a gutter width of ¼". This is very similar to most books found in the LDS market of this type and size.

[Rachel] I must admit that BJ's self-published books really are typeset well, so I don't have anything else to add. Good job!

COVER DESIGN AND LAYOUT

[BJ[This is probably the most demanding step involved in the production of your book. Creating the perfect design—one that best represents your book and will attract buyers—is a daunting challenge. Take a close look at other books on the market, and get a feel for what works and what doesn't. Typically you want to tackle the artwork or photography at a professional level, which means you need a graphic design software package such as Adobe PhotoShop. Once the artwork is complete, you may want to do the actual layout with similar software as that used for your typesetting. Some design packages do both.

[Rachel] Doing your cover yourself is best for personal creative control (or you might have a family member who can do it for you), but you can pay a professional to do any part of a cover, from taking a picture to designing the whole thing. Of course, that kind of help

costs money, but if cover design is not something you feel that you can do or have time for, hiring someone is a good choice. You can still maintain design control and ask for changes along the way. Keep in mind that professional software programs for designing covers are expensive, and if self-publishing is a one-time thing for you, it might be less expensive to hire out the work.

[BJ] In addition to standard four-color presswork, other options typically used for both soft- and hard-cover books include foil stamping, gold or silver ink, and blind embossing. Your printer should be able to assist you in preparing your files for those embellishments. Whenever feasible, pay to include embossing on your cover. Your book will really stand out!

Like the rest of your book, the finished cover design should be copied to a CD or ZipDisk, along with all applicable fonts and images, to be delivered to the printer.

The background cover art for all of my books was done with Adobe Photoshop, saved in high resolution TIFF format, and imported into a QuarkXpress file for the final layout. The covers were printed on a four-color offset press.

LEGAL REQUIREMENTS

To sell your book in most retail establishments, it must have an ISBN number assigned to it, which must be included in both numeric and barcode format on the back cover or on the jacket cover of your book. This number also appears on the copyright page. ISBN numbers can be purchased in blocks of 10, 100, 1000, or even 10,000, through R.R. Bowker. Forms are available at: **www.bowkerlink.com**. (The printing company produces the barcode for you once you provide them with the ISBN number and the appropriate white space on your cover design. There are also online services that can produce them fairly inexpensively.)

Right away—as soon as the book comes off the press—you need to send two copies, with a small fee, to the Library of Congress to register your copyright. The forms, instructions, and answers to questions are available online at: **www.copyright.gov**.

And there you are . . . a pallet-load of first-class, quality books is delivered to your door, with the whole world waiting anxiously to sample and taste your exquisite pie for themselves.

Now, go out there and market, market, market!

Here's some handy reference material that has been very useful to me:

Self-Editing For Fiction Writers: How to Edit Yourself into Print by Renni Browne and Dave King, HarperPerennial, 1994

The Self-Publishing Manual: How to Write, Print, and Sell Your Own Book, 14th Edition; by Dan Poynter (Paperback), Para Publishing, 2003

chapter 10

Thinking Outside the Bookstore

Self-Promotion

by Shirley Bahlmann

with contributions by
Anne Bradshaw & Marsha Ward

Your book is written and published. You have arrived! Now all you have to do is sit back and wait for royalties to roll in.

Or, with that approach, "dribble in" is more like it.

Even if your publisher does promotion for you, no one can push your book like you can. There is no other person on planet Earth who cares about the success of your book as much as you do. Your enthusiasm will shine when you personally promote the paper and ink extension of your heart and soul.

The first thing to do is tell people that you wrote a book. It's easy to bring up in conversation. I keep half-page flyers with me, printed on attention-grabbing neon colored paper, to give to those who express an interest in my books. The flyers include pictures of my book covers with brief descriptions, a couple of endorsements, and a website to visit for more information.

[Anne] Don't overlook the power of frugal LDS readers who would rather borrow books than buy them. Their enthusiasm for your writing can spill into the neighborhood when your book makes

its rounds. Your novel is sure to spark interest in a few who will decide to buy a copy of their own. A new neighbor recently bought two of my books. Her parting words were, "As soon as I've finished reading, I'll pass them on to my mother. She loves this kind of book." I mentally tagged on, "and your sisters, aunts, cousins, and grandparents." But hey, that's okay! It's still getting the word out. Publicity comes in unpredictable packages.

[Marsha] Something I do when I hand-sell my books is to give buyers as many bookmarks or postcards that feature my book as I can, for them to hand out to their friends and relatives. I find the best price available on the Internet for these items, and order them by the thousands—literally. They are a great investment of my promotional dollars.

In addition to handing them out to buyers and handing them out at events, I send out bookmarks in every piece of mail that leaves my house, bill payments included. Postcards go out to my mailing list when each book is released.

You do *have a mailing list, don't you? Compile a list of the people who buy books from you, or who visit your website, or who express interest in your writing.*

Speaking of mailing, I use 1" x 2 5/8" mailing labels to help publicize my books. Last Christmas I printed my book information and website on these stickers and put them on the back flap of my Christmas cards. These also go on every piece of mail I send. If you have only one book, consider printing an eye-catching, albeit small, graphic of your book cover—in color—on the label.

In addition to a mailing list, you can compile an e-mail list for electronic announcements of your book and accomplishments. Start with your current address book. Invite people to sign the guest book at your website (set one up, if you don't already have one) and make sure there is a box for their e-mail address.

Join as many online listservers, communities, and groups as you can handle, both for writers and readers of the type of book you write. Participate. Ask and answer questions. Make friends. Become a known entity. It won't be strange, then, when you announce the birth of your baby book.

[Shirley] Book signings are a great way to get to know store managers and employees, who, once they meet you, will be able to put a face with your book, and are more likely to recommend it to potential buyers. Most publishers line up book signings for you, but I have succeeded in contacting bookstores and making my own appointments to autograph books when planning a trip or vacation. I give them enough advance notice that they can order books from my publisher. I take books with me in case they run out, and on occasion they have asked me to bring my newest release.

I hand out my half-page flyers at book signings also. I make the flyers with my own computer and scanner. I scan the book covers into Microsoft Publisher, then add a description of the books, endorsements, and ordering information. It has to be brief, but I always include my website so they can refer to it when they get home. I have had people take a flyer with them, then come back to my signing table minutes later, flyer in hand, to purchase a book.

I used to be rather aggressive in handing out the flyers. When there was no one close to my signing table, I would even follow people down the book aisles to hand them out. I no longer do that. I felt that it put some people off, and wasted a lot of flyers.

Now I lay the flyers on the signing table within easy reach of passers-by and sit down with a project in hand, such as making notes for a current book or reading. When people walk by, I look up, smile, and say, "Hi." If the customers are interested in what I'm doing, they'll come over. If not, they don't feel threatened. They've seen my poster, and perhaps they'll remember me later with fondness instead of dread!

[Marsha] Think of other places where you can sign your books—especially places that correlate to your book's theme. How about historical and genealogical societies? Feed and seed stores? Beauty shops, gift shops, restaurants with gift shops, restaurants that cater to your target audience? Riding stables, ice cream shops, pet stores—the list is endless. Use your imagination and find alternative locations for book signings.

The upside of many of these is that the owner may not charge you a percentage of your book sales! I found a small café named Grandma's Kitchen *whose proprietor agreed to let me sell books during her breakfast hours. I put up posters, sent out postcards, and left counter cards at the location. The owner donated the breakfast beverage. I had a good time and sold several books.*

[Shirley] A great way to advertise your wares is to get some air time on radio or television. Many radio stations have interview formats and may be happy to have you as a guest on their show. It is good marketing strategy to offer a certain number of your books for the station to give away as promotional items. Radio station listings are available on the Internet or in phone books.

When you have your interview, think only of speaking to the person who is asking you questions rather than picturing in your mind all the people who might be listening. Make yourself more comfortable by concentrating on talking one-on-one to the radio announcer. See him as a person who is interested in what you wrote. Have brief notes on the main points you want to cover and work them into the broadcast. You can answer the announcer's question, then bring up a topic you'd like to address. It's your book. You're in charge.

You can even get yourself a television spot. Find an unusual angle or a seasonal complement to what you write, then polish up a proposal and send it to television stations. Better yet, make an appointment with the program director and pitch your proposal in person.

Since my *Odds* series is about pioneers, I was able to garner a spot on Channel 4's "Good Things Utah" on July 23rd. I pitched my books as "pioneer stories with attitude!" That got the interest of the station manager, I got my two-and-a-half minutes, and had a blast doing it! I focused on the two women who interviewed me, imagining them as interested passers-by at my book-signing table, and didn't even give a thought to the thousands of people tuned in to the show.

There's something to be said for getting from point A to point B along the same old tried and true path, but it's also important to sometimes let your mind wander over the less traveled fields of your imagination. You can find some creative marketing ideas hiding in the tall grass if you aren't afraid to explore.

For example, I offer an assembly featuring my pioneer stories to schools. At first, I decided to charge a fee and offer my books at a discount. After a couple of assemblies, however, I got the idea to offer schools the option to either pay my fee, or send flyers home with their students, which feature my books at a discount price. If school faculty and student families order a minimum number of books, then I do the assembly at no additional cost. I get my fee from the sales, readers get a great book, schools have a supplement to their Utah History studies, and everybody's happy. I have managed to get press releases in local papers, but you need to write these with the paper's readers in mind, rather than as a sole promotion of your book. If it's self-aggrandizing, it may be viewed as an advertisement, and will be rejected. Again, get your creative juices going on the subject of how you can present your work in a way that will benefit readers and the publisher.

A book dealing with a past war can accompany an article with a topic of goodwill for mankind. For a book dealing with the mentally ill, your article can mention ways that mentally ill people can be valued and accepted in the community. If you have a story on mothers, you can focus on the bond between a mother and her children, and how important it is for people to nurture that bond in appropriate ways.

[Anne] Another idea is to approach as many libraries as you can find, both local and countrywide. Getting a magazine such as Library Journal *to review your book is a bonus. This publication is fundamental reading for librarians, acting as a basis for future orders. If you contact libraries, pointing out the review, and stating the exact issue and page number, your chance of being chosen is increased.*

Library e-mail addresses can be found on the Internet by doing a Google search for libraries public Utah *(or whichever state you choose). It can be a lengthy process, but worthwhile. The borrowing public may recommend your books to others who wish to buy—or even purchase copies for themselves.*

[Shirley] Take your book to places that don't ordinarily carry books. I have a couple of small gas station convenience stores that sell a phenomenal number of my books, especially in the tourist season. If your publisher allows you to market your own books, offer a percentage of the cover price to the establishment in exchange for their carrying your books and ringing up sales. Make sure it's not such a steep discount that it isn't worth your time and effort to re-supply them.

When you address the manager, smile. Be enthusiastic and upbeat about what you have to offer. Tell them this is in their best interest, as it will make them X number of dollars just for ringing up a sale. If you offer it on a consignment basis, most will usually agree, although not everyone will say yes. Try beauty salons, sporting goods stores, hobby shops—whatever strikes your interest.

Putting books in places where people have to wait is a good strategy. I have some of mine at Salt Lake Monument, where headstones are made for cemeteries. One day, two families were there at the same time ordering stones. By the time both families got finished, another man, who'd been waiting and passing the time looking at one of my books, said, "Now I'll have to buy this to see how the story ends."

Make it like a treasure hunt, with people discovering your book as the ultimate find! Keep records of what worked and what didn't.

[Anne] An idea that worked for me is selling copies of my books on Deseret Book Auctions and on eBay. LDS books sell best on Deseret Book Auctions, of course, and if you don't mind the chore of managing your own shipping, it's fun to see where your books go. I have kept a record of every book sent out and to where. Terracotta Summer *and* Chamomile Winter *have spread all over the USA and Britain—and are still spreading!*

You access the auctions by clicking the Mormonlife link at ***www.deseretbook.com****. You must join Mormonlife to participate, but there is no cost to join. Use the password you choose at joining for access to the Auction page via a link at the top of the Mormonlife page.*

Instructions for adding items to auctions are easy to follow. You can use HTML to enhance descriptions. Then choose Paypal or another method of payment such as checks or money orders.

You select your own shipping costs. I keep mine down, as I think it attracts more bids. I also keep the starting bid reasonably low. Often bids never reach the book cover price, but that's okay because my books sell together, and it is a chance to introduce the sequel and to do more promoting. I include a couple of bookmarks with details of my work in each signed copy. You never know who will receive them.

Sometimes you can buy scratch-and-dent copies of your books from your publisher at a reasonable cost. The damage is often minor enough to go unnoticed by the average reader. This makes it possible to give an attractive low starting price in an auction.

If no one bids on your item, you are not charged anything. Your first listed item is free. Thereafter, you are entitled to free listings each week, depending on your feedback rating. Deseret Book charges for listings only when all your freebies are used up—then it's 25¢ per auction. For the buyer it costs nothing to register, bid, or win.

There's a small closing fee charged if your book sells, which is a percentage of the final bid—i.e. for a book that sells for $25 or under, the percentage is 5% with a maximum of $1.25. Any fees accumulated during the month are charged to your credit card the following month.

So far, I've had just under one hundred sales relating directly or indirectly to these auctions, and am pleased with the many positive comments that have come back regarding my stories. Only one bidder took forever to pay. (Never send any book until the check has cleared, by the way.) The others have been superb winners who leave excellent feedback, which builds your reputation as a seller, increasing your chance of sales. This you need, because Deseret auctions have grown in size, and competition is high.

[Shirley] Look into local and regional events where you might set up a table and offer your books to people. They may not know they could benefit from something new to read while they wait—until you tell them. I live close to Manti, home of the *Mormon Miracle Pageant.* I usually sign quite a few books there.

I've also been to the *Handcart Pageant* in Nephi, and *This Is The Place Monument State Park* during their Civil War days. You could sell your books at rodeos, piano recitals, club meetings, county fairs, and more. And don't forget those annual family reunions. Let your imagination run, and don't discard any ideas. You may come up with a whole new angle that no one has ever thought of before.

When you're at your station, smile, and be enthused! Yet keep in mind that not everyone is interested in reading your book. Some people would rather sit in front of the TV and watch *Gilligan's Island* re-runs.

It's impossible to write a book everyone will like. Knowing this, you can take rejection in stride, and look beyond the people saying, "No thanks," to the next person in line. Your book may be just what they're looking for.

I once gave a talk at a library. Due to inadequate advertising, only the librarian and her assistant attended, plus a couple of people they pulled off computers to listen to me speak! In spite of the small audience, I gave them my best and ended up selling six books.

[Marsha] I've had quite a bit of success giving talks to Friends of the Library groups. A favorite topic with such groups is "Is the Western Dead? Books, Movies, and More." At a talk in Payson, Arizona, one woman called her husband, saying, "Get dressed and come down here quick. She's going to talk about Westerns." I sold them a book afterward. Another woman knew the topic and invited her husband to come along to the meeting. They, too, bought a book, as did many other people in attendance.

I got another booking as a direct result of that appearance. A Library Friends' group in another community hosts an annual fund-raising "Silver Tea," but their guest speaker ended up in the hospital and cancelled. Among the groups the organizer called was the one in Payson, who mentioned that I had been a recent speaker. I was delighted to take a trip to that community, give a revised version of the same talk, and sell a healthy number of my books.

[Shirley] Let community, Church, and school groups know you're available to give talks. Make the talk fit the occasion. If it's for Church, you could talk about fulfilling your purpose on earth and magnifying talents. Listeners will become familiar with your name and look up your books later. (But remember, it's not appropriate to sell books at a Church function.)

If it's for youth, encourage them to follow their dreams, set goals, and never give up.

If the topic and venue are appropriate, discuss your book with your listeners. A lot of people like to hear about your journey from wanna-be to published author. Talk with whoever is in charge of the meeting and see what topic they would like to have you address. Then give it an outline, run through it a couple of times, say your prayers, and rely on inspiration. You may give several listeners the encouragement they need at a particular time in their lives, and they won't forget you.

See if there is a business or company that you can pair your books with. For example, if you write a romance, you could offer it to a floral company at a discount to go with a bouquet for Valentine's Day, Mother's Day, or birthdays. It's a unique combination that could prove good for you and good for them. You're a writer; think creatively!

Think of other places or events that match your type of book. Imagine ways in which your books and their services could be combined, and approach them with this idea in mind. They won't all say yes, but the ones who do, who are creative enough to try something new, will be the ones you want to work with anyway.

Most of all, believe in what you do, regardless of what anyone else says. Don't let anyone rain on your parade. March out at the front of the line, and let the world know your book is available and worth reading!

chapter 11

Mind Your Own Business!

Writing as a Legitimate Career

by Josi Kilpack

with contributions by
BJ Rowley & Shirley Bahlmann

The non-writing people of the world seem to have a difficult time looking at writing as anything other than a mere hobby—something to be tinkered with, at best. I remember watching a TV sitcom some time ago where two people were asking this guy what he did for a living. He answered proudly that he was a writer. The two looked at one another, smiled, and said in unison, "Unemployed."

R - E - S - P - E - C - T

Why is it so hard for people to accept writing as a serious pursuit? Even when looking at famous authors, the likes of Stephen King, Amy Tan, and John Grisham, people often feel these guys were just lucky enough to have turned a hobby into a successful financial venture.

[BJ] Yeah, kind of like inheriting a fortune from a rich uncle. Sheer luck.

[Shirley] Some people, when they hear that someone works at home writing books, get a look on their face as if they'd just been told that Marshmallow Stacking is the newest Olympic event. They don't believe that writing could possibly be a valid profession. It ranks in their minds on the same scale as watching TV and eating bon bons. Perhaps because a book can be picked up and easily read in a few hours, such people discount the days and weeks and months that went into getting that story down on paper in the first place. Or maybe they don't find value in books at all.

[Josi] It's up to you, the writer, to set the tone of your career. If you treat what you do as a hobby—something disposable that can be done any time and isn't important enough to make time for—everyone around you will treat it that way, too. You need to decide what it is for *you*. If it *is* just a hobby, fit it in where you can, speak of it casually, and focus on the fun of it. But if writing is a career, part of the lifeblood that makes you *you*, the first person who needs to know that is you.

One way is to "clock in," just as you would at the office. I have experimented with many ways of doing this. As a mostly stay-at-home mom, I have a certain level of flexibility—or so everyone assumes. The truth is that it's incredibly hard to keep a train of thought together while getting bombarded with snack requests, dirty diapers, car pools, concert dates, and phone calls. I've tried staying up late to write, I've tried waking up early—neither works well for long. I need my sleep!

What I *have* found that works is to choose a chunk of time during the day to write, and prepare in advance. My best time is from 9:00 to 11:00 in the morning. Three of my four kids are in school during this time. I get my two-year-old ready for the day, she helps me clean her room, then I fill up a bottle, give her the binky and her favorite doll, and put on a movie. Once I make sure her basic needs are met, I get to work. I still get up for her once or twice, but when I set aside this time consistently, she accepts it as part of her routine.

I don't like to write when my older kids are home, and I try not to write when my husband comes home from work, either, although it's hard not to when I have storylines and characters screaming at me, demanding my attention. A lot of writers turn off the phone when they write, but if my kids aren't home, I hate cutting that line of communication. I *do* watch my caller ID.

Outside of my scheduled time, I grab ten minutes here and fifteen minutes there throughout the day. On a good day I can write 3,000 words, and as long as I'm progressing, I feel good.

On the other hand, there are times when I just can't write. I work part-time, two days a week. I don't get any writing done on work days. Often I go for weeks without writing anything, although I try not to, as it really gets me out of my groove.

However you schedule your time, treat it seriously. Always listen to the Spirit for any promptings on balancing your life and giving service, of course. But generally speaking, if someone calls and wants you to watch their kids during your writing time, say no. When you schedule appointments, schedule around it. Don't let yourself be bullied. Your visiting or home teachers don't have to come during that sacred writing time. Would they come to your office while you were on the clock? Not likely. Writing time deserves the same respect as a traditional job.

Let the answering machine or voice mail be your best friend. Train yourself that unless it's the school calling to say your child is ill, you honestly do not have to pick up the telephone. Learn to let it ring, if you don't already. If you don't have caller ID, it's worth every penny and then some—especially since many people don't leave messages. Think of it this way: a ringing phone means it was a convenient time for someone to pick up *their* phone and call *you*. You are not obligated to pick it up if your hands are full, which includes fingers typing furiously on a keyboard. Return calls at *your* convenience.

You may work full-time and have to schedule writing time around your job. Talk to your family and find times that work. Let them know how important their support is to you. If you don't carve out the time, no one else will. Your writing has to be a priority or it will be lost among the urgencies of life.

[Shirley] I rarely watch TV or videos. When my family is watching a movie, I'll usually run to the computer and get in some valuable writing time.

[BJ] Like most guys, I do *work full-time. In fact, when someone asks me what I do for a living, I usually answer, "During the day, or at night and weekends?" Then I see that pained look in their eyes, like they're thinking, "Oh, poor sap. Holding down two jobs!" When I tell them I moonlight as a writer, their face relaxes and that "oh-you-mean-your-hobby" look comes over them. Everybody has time for a hobby. That's no big deal.*

But carving out time for quality writing is a serious challenge for me—a daunting task. During the past several years, I've done a fair amount of traveling as part of my job. I've discovered that some of my best writing takes place in the evening, in hotel rooms, when there's no one around to interrupt. Talk about quality time! It did take awhile to discipline myself not to touch that tempting TV remote, but it's well worth the sacrifice.

When I'm not traveling, late nights work best for me, especially on weekends when I don't have to get up early the next day. I can easily glue myself to my chair and spend literally hours losing myself in the adventures of my characters.

At other times, as Josi suggested, I have to carve out a specific time and label it official writing time. In fact, when my kids were all teenagers and still at home demanding my attention, I posted a sign outside my closed office door that read. "Genius At Work—Do Not Disturb!" They learned real quick that Daddy would get quite grumpy if his creative moments were needlessly interrupted. They came to realize that it was serious time—my writing career time, my work—and they respected me for that. I made sure to set aside plenty of time for them also—an equally important priority.

[Shirley] What works best for me is to keep a daily writing log. Some writers use a blank monthly or weekly planning calendar. Instead of writing appointments in the squares, they keep track of the writing they do each day—their writing time, the number of pages, or the number of words, depending on the personal goals

they set for themselves. You can make a brief note of the project you're working on, any significant happenings or contacts in your writing life, and any phone calls received or made regarding your writing business. The entries need not be lengthy. A simple note to remind you of what you did or who you spoke to is sufficient.

Keeping track of your writing accomplishments can validate you as one who takes the job seriously, and it's a real pick-me-up when you feel like you have made no progress at all. You can look back at your record and see that two weeks ago you had absolutely nothing written on your new book, and now you're fifty pages into it. The warmth of accomplishment can be enough to spur you on to a fresh burst of creativity.

Above all, take your own work seriously. Don't set it aside for minor distractions. Obviously, a family member in need is worthy of your attention. Follow your heart. Beware the guilty prodding of whiners on the phone, those who failed to plan ahead and try to lay their unfinished burdens on your shoulders. Beware also of bored friends who can take up valuable writing time in idle chit-chat because "you're just sitting at home doing nothing important."

[BJ] This reminds me of the old saying: "Failure to plan on your part does not constitute an emergency on my part."

MONEY

[Josi] John Steinbeck once said, "The profession of book writing makes horse racing seem like a solid, stable business."

Inspiring, isn't it?

Seriously though, he has a point. After you write a book, then work and slave over rewrites, it seems high time for the money to roll in. For a few very lucky individuals this might happen, but those few are mostly published in the national market.

Throughout this book we've pointed out the difference between the national and LDS markets, and we'll do the same here. Authors are paid royalties on books sold. A royalty is a percentage of the sales paid to the author. Most authors in the

LDS market are getting from 5-15% of the selling price. The publisher establishes the cover (retail) price. The contract terms determine whether author royalties are based on the wholesale price (generally 60% of retail) or the retail price itself. This is an important distinction.

If the royalty is based on retail, it is likely to come in at around 6-8%. If the author royalty is based on the wholesale price, it should fall closer to 10-12%. Either way winds up about the same amount earned per book, in theory. You must remember that the wholesale price is a variable. The retail price is printed right on the cover and is much less in question. Consider the possibility that if your contract is for, say, 10% of the wholesale selling price, and the publisher sells 500 copies at a deep discount, your royalty is equally discounted on each of those 500 copies.

Some contracts use terms like *net receipts* or *gross receipts* to indicate wholesale selling price. Either way, it's vital to get the publisher to clarify exactly how they define those terms and do their accounting.

Royalties based on retail (or cover price), are far less confusing to account for on your royalty statements. Some authors have received statements as simple as "1485 books sold = $526.92," with no explanation whatsoever as to how the publisher's accounting department came up with that number. Whereas, when an author knows her royalty is a constant 6% of $14.95, multiplied by 1000 copies (that's $897.00 in this example), it's easy to figure out at home whether the check is correct.

A few LDS publishers are known to set their royalties on a sliding scale based on number of copies sold, increasing the royalty percentage after, say, 1000 or 5000 copies are sold. Be sure that you understand exactly what your royalty terms mean before you sign a contract.

Your publisher should provide you with a detailed royalty statement, including the number of books sold at each price or variable royalty amount, especially if the contract is based on the wholesale price. Many of us can attest that good statements can sometimes be difficult to obtain. Usually the right to receive an accurate statement is included in the contract terms, along with the author's right to have an audit performed.

Say your book sells for $14.95, you earn about 90¢ a book. That means, after selling 1,000 copies, you earn about $900. This is a discouraging discovery for some writers. But if you write more books, and your sales continue to grow, it is possible to make a living with your writing—eventually.

Many first-time authors sell around 2,500 copies of their first book their first year. Some can sell four or five times that amount. Very few authors in the LDS market sell more than 10,000 copies in the first year, unless it's a non-fiction book with particular interest, a hardback novel the publisher has chosen to put most of their advertising dollar behind, or an author with a very large following. Every new book an author publishes helps sell additional copies of their preceding books—their "backlist."

You have likely heard of "advances." Although they exist in the LDS market from time to time, they are not the norm and are only offered to established authors whom publishers know will sell many thousands of copies. Another thing to understand is that an advance is exactly that—an advance. It's not a retainer, not a bonus, not a salary. You get paid in advance against royalties that are expected to be earned.

For example, should you be advanced $2,000, you won't see any *more* money until the advance is earned out by selling enough of your books to cover that amount in royalties. Only then would you receive additional royalties, as more books sell. That's a *lot* of books. The LDS market is small, and if sales go over 10,000, that's a huge bestseller.

But you *can* expect royalties.

Every publisher pays differently, but none that I'm aware of pay anything for at least six months following the release of your book. The reason for this is that once a book is ordered by a bookstore, orders have to be processed, books shipped and placed on the shelf, and then the bookstore has two or three months to pay the publisher.

If your publisher uses an outside distributor, it can take twice that long for the books and money to make the rounds.

On top of all that, there are often returns for damaged, unsold, or over-purchased books. Publishers allow six months from the point of sale before they pay you.

Generally, the LDS market pays in royalties rather than in an advance. Every publisher pays those royalties as they choose. Some pay every month on a six-month delay, meaning you get paid in June for books sold in December, in July for books sold in January, and so on. Other publishers pay quarterly, with the same six-month time cushion, meaning you would be paid for the first quarter of the year (January-March) the following October. Some publishers pay twice a year—in early February for sales from July through December, and then again in early August for sales from January through June. Your payment schedule should be outlined in your contract.

Now that you understand how the money works, what do you do with it once you get it? Well, there are many options. I have a separate account from my household accounts to use for all my book income and expenses. Whatever you do, make sure you keep all your statements.

[BJ] Your publisher should send you a form 1099 at the end of the year, detailing the amount of money paid to you in royalties. Your tax accountant can easily add this to your regular tax forms, without the need for extensive paperwork. If you have deductible expenses from your writing, then you'll want to complete a "Schedule C," where your earnings and expenses can be detailed and deducted. I know an author who does a lot of book signings, and since she keeps records of all the miles that she drives in connection with her writing, she was able to deduct $1,000 just for mileage.

[Shirley] File the receipts that you get for items that you buy for your writing business. This includes paper, pencils, pens, printer ink cartridges, postage to mail books or letters having to do with your writing, envelopes, gas to and from signings or publicity events, and telephone calls for the purpose of advancing your writing career.

[Josi] It might be a good idea to talk to an accountant and see what advice they may have to offer. The bottom line is, even if you don't write for the money, you still need to take care of it. Regardless of how much or how little you make, there is nothing more validating than seeing a book you wrote in print.

It's exciting and addicting. And in time that addiction to writing—that need to create—can make you some fairly decent money.

When it comes in, track it carefully and manage it wisely.

You're Kidding, Right?

Things They Never Tell You

by Shirley Bahlmann

with contributions by
Julie Wright & Josi Kilpack

At last, the long, drawn-out publishing process is complete. You have your book in hand, the glossy cover boasting your name in bold letters.

You prop your masterpiece up on the entryway table and leaf through a stack of cruise brochures, deciding which one you'll take with your first royalty check. You glance around the room and decide that the second royalty check will go toward new furniture and a complete house make-over.

The phone is annoyingly silent. When is Oprah going to call and beg you to be her featured guest?

[Julie] In fact, you're considering putting her off for a month just to show her that you have posture. After all, it might be tacky to appear too eager.

[Shirley] You picture the mailman emptying his mailbag through the mail slot in your door. The pile of letters will be full of congratulations and well wishes from your family, friends, and neighbors. Some ask for autographs, some ask for photos, and some request autographed photos of you holding up your book.

You imagine your publisher running out of your first printing in one day, necessitating a rush job on a second printing in order to fill the incredible demand for your book.

Hey, you may as well skip the house make-over and just buy an all-new one, say, a mansion. If you're going to be an author, then by golly, you're going to live like one!

Stop. Rewind. Back to reality.

At last, you have your book in hand, with your name in big, bold letters on the cover. You flip through the pages. It's perfect. Absolutely per— Wait! What's this? A typo? A mistake? You stare at the traitor word, your heart pounding.

How could this be? You know you didn't write it like that! Your story was absolute perfection when you sent off your galleys. How could it become scarred in such a short time?

In a panic, you scan the pages. Oh, no! There's another blemish! A capital letter printed in lower case! And the italics are missing from the first page on chapter three! The *-ing* was left off the word *match* on page 157, and makes you look like a grammatical idiot!

You fall back against your chair and stare wide-eyed at the ceiling. How could this happen? You reach for the phone and call your publisher. "There are mistakes!" you cry.

You're promptly reminded that you *were* given the galley proofs for final approval, and you sent it back to the publisher with your changes marked in red. They made your changes. If you didn't catch something . . . well . . . they'll see about fixing it in the second printing.

They are clearly not as worried as you are about the scars in your book. With a shaking hand, you replace the telephone receiver.

You shuffle through your mail. Bills, bills, bills, and a craft magazine. Oh wait, there's a . . . no, that isn't for you. It's a letter for your daughter from the missionary she was planning on dumping the next time she wrote.

As for the cruise, you may have to plan that for several years down the road. It might be wise to add any loose change you find under the couch cushions to your cruise fund, since you won't receive royalties for six months.

Thus begin the things they never tell you about publishing.

[Julie] Some of the shock is from being a novice and not really understanding the contract. And where a writer might have easily understood, he or she might have been too excited to really care what's in the contract.

This was the case with me. I was so pleased to sign that I failed to read the contract. Once my book hit the publisher's bestsellers list three months in a row and I still didn't have a royalty check, I got annoyed enough to call the accountant, who was displeased with the illiteracy of this writer and told me to go back and read my contract.

Reading my contract was a lightbulb moment. I learned how long I'd have to wait for my first and subsequent paychecks, what my pay scale was, and how often I would be paid.

[Josi] The arrival of your royalty check is the moment that defines why you really wrote what you wrote and worked as hard as you did. If it was for the money, chances are you'd never write again. But now that you've read this book, you'll know better.

[Shirley] For most LDS authors, the best you can expect from book royalties is a little extra pocket money.

This is not to say you won't get rich by writing books, but it's not to say you won't be struck by a meteor on your way home from the drugstore, either. For the most people, it just doesn't happen. (Check out Chapter Eleven, *Writing as a Legitimate Career*, for more on how royalties work.)

Fast forward.

Your book has been out for a week or two, word has gotten around the neighborhood that you have actually written a book, and you find yourself standing in line in the grocery store. There's a neighbor lady waiting behind you.

"Hey, I heard you wrote a book," she says.

"Yes," you answer, blushing with modest pride.

She narrows her eyes at you. "Was it a children's book?" (Why is it that most people believe writing a children's book is as easy as a bubble bath, when it's actually very difficult to wrangle with the economy of words that picture books require?)

"No, it's a novel," you say.

"A whole novel?"

"Yes."

She leans forward. "Did you really write it all by yourself?"

[Julie] The incredulity of others shouldn't offend you. It shouldn't, but sometimes it does. A friend was at my parent's house at the same time I was, and he mentioned that he was writing a book. I smiled and said, "Oh really? Me, too."

His expression flattened into bored irritation, and he said, "No. You don't understand. I really am."

Puzzled at this, I straightened. "I really am, too. I just finished my first novel, and it should be in the stores in just a few weeks."

"You did not."

"I did too!"

"And someone actually published it?"

For this there is no politically correct reply. You can either get angry and vocal or angry and quiet. I'm the quiet angry type, so I fumed over it until humor struck me. This friend is a great person—someone I truly care for. But he still hasn't made it past page thirty in the book that he is "really" writing, and therefore is not in the position to judge what I have done. To let that mar the friendship would be unthinkable.

[Shirley] Of course there *are* people who will congratulate you on your accomplishment, and your friends and family who will smile and hug you and buy two copies of your book so they can give one away as a gift. Many well-wishers have genuine interest in the success of your ventures.

Yet behind some of those smiles lurks a smattering of jealousy. Behind others is a great green wall of envy.

The following is a collection of experiences of real authors who received an unexpected wake-up call after their first book was published:

> "I thought people would be so excited and impressed, but it's not that way."
>
> "Some of my friends and family have been very supportive, but others have been jealous. One friend feels that I'm leaving her behind in what I'm doing. Now that I have an outside career and new friends, she feels that she is just not as important as I am, and thinks that my success diminishes her self-worth. It hurts her feelings when I talk about my signings and other fun things I get to do. It has put a damper on our relationship because I don't feel like I can talk to her about my career, and so our conversations are stilted and unnatural."
>
> "A lot of people seem to treat me like I just got lucky. They don't seem to think I'm really all that good. Even though it's just their opinion, it still bites."
>
> "Some relatives of ours have taken my success pretty hard. At first they acted cold toward me and said, 'Let us know when you make your first million.' I explained to them that writing for the LDS market doesn't turn out millionaires. Then they said, 'Well, can't you write anything else?' So at first they were miffed that I was going to be rich, and now they're miffed that I'm not."
>
> "It gets embarrassing when people call me 'famous.' I imagine that there might be jealous people out there, but if so, I don't recognize them. I usually have on my rose-colored glasses.

I probably wouldn't believe it even if they said, 'I'm jealous of you.' I'd think they were just teasing."

"I believe people do get very envious, even if they won't consciously admit it to themselves. Those who can be truly happy for you are your real friends. The rest can become the bad guys in your next book."

"[*A well-known author*] is in my stake. He was very happy for me when my book was accepted, and when we see each other in the hall when wards change places he'll ask me how things are going. On the other hand, there is another ward member who seems to have a hard time handling what I have done. Whenever she hears someone mention my book, she immediately tells all within ear shot that I am not the only author in the stake, and that [*the well-known author*] is much more successful, since he's published nine books."

"My book was displayed recently on a table at our stake Relief Society conference. It's been out about three years, and a few sisters in my ward that I know fairly well came up and said, 'Wow, I didn't know you wrote a book!' I must be terrible at PR, even though I do talk about my book at the slightest provocation."

"I have several friends (close ones, I thought) and family members who have never read my books. They'll say they want to, but they never do. These are often those that 'have a book in them,' and I can feel their jealously ooze all over the place when someone talks about my book. It's very sad. If they ever published, I would read it first thing."

"It all goes with that 'a prophet is without honor in his own country' business."

"I think some people hesitate to pick up your book and read it if they know you, even though it's been officially published. How many times have you had someone hand you a story or poem they wrote, and it completely stinks, and then you have to act nice about it? I make sure to tell people they don't have to like it. You don't have to say nice things to me if you hate it. I can take it. Who knows whether they listen?"

"The hardest thing for me has been the general attitude about the way people are treating me. I have tried so hard not to act any differently than I did before. I don't bring up my books; I don't even talk about it unless someone asks a question. But those around me act as though I'm different. It's on their minds whenever they see me, so they tend to make it much larger than it already is. Even though I'm not acting like a celebrity snob, people treat me like I'm acting that way."

"Only two of my sisters haven't read my books. One doesn't read them because she doesn't enjoy reading and can only do it in short spurts with total quiet. She's always been that way, and I understand. She happens to be one of my best cheerleaders. The other sister doesn't read them or tell me 'good job' either. I am not offended by this in the least."

"The best compliment I received was from both my own daughter and another close friend: 'It was so *good*, I forgot you wrote it!' I took it exactly as intended. They were so caught up in the story that it wasn't like, 'Here I am reading Mom's book because I have to.' It was as good as anything they'd read by Famous People."

"One of my cousins looked at my novel and said, 'Whoa! That's more writing than I'd do in my whole life!' "

"A brother and sister actually said that I have been a motivating example for them to have the courage to go after their dreams and believe that they'll achieve them."

[Shirley] Some of us have experienced the over-bearing offers from acquaintances who want to re-work our books for us, eager to point out where all the faults lie and how we could write a much better book with their supervision.

It seems that the best tactic to deal with the discontents is to urge them to write their own books instead of dabbling in yours. (That way, they could start fresh to create their own perfection. My prediction is that they'll never finish a book in their whole life.)

In the case of someone who seems to resent you for what you've done, it may be wise to just avoid discussing your writing projects with them. Keep the conversation on neutral topics.

Above all, respect their right to their feelings. Keep your cool. Be kind. Try to relate to them. After all, you may have had some of those same inklings in the time before your book was published. Dig into your writer's soul and pull out a double handful of empathy.

There seems to be a prevailing attitude in our culture that women shouldn't have interests outside the home.

[Josi] It seems that if we do, we're breaking some kind of commandment. The reality is that we have been told time after time to pursue our interests, increase our knowledge, and strengthen our talents. If writing is the talent and passion that

you've been blessed with, then I feel you are under obligation to find out how the Lord expects you to use it and develop it. Not only does it broaden your horizons, but it sets an example of accomplishment and continual growth and education for your children. I know I'm a better mother because I write. I have had several Church callings that have drawn upon my writing, and I am able to share my testimony through my words.

Even though I didn't have a lifelong dream of becoming a published author, I know I am where the Lord wants me to be. It's hard to balance family and career. It's tricky to cover all the bases, but I'm here for a reason, and He knows it. If I work hard to fulfill my responsibilities, He helps me find time for my writing. It's a great arrangement.

[Julie] Another constant attitude I battle is when people don't understand that being a writer is a serious thing, and that I need time to write. There are times when someone will volunteer me for something, thinking that I have loads of extra time because all I do is sit around the house and write. They treat it like a hobby when it is my profession. I've had to learn to let people know that I can't do all the things they think I can because writing is something that must be done. There are deadlines and schedules that must be followed if I am ever to succeed.

[Shirley] Not only are there some changes you may not have imagined occurring in your private life, but when you go out to promote your book, you will most likely come face to face with a whole new set of "I can't believe this!" events. There are authors who have shown up for book signings, and the store doesn't have any of their books on hand. It's also a very real possibility that once you're set up, none of the customers will even come within shouting distance of your table.

On the other hand, some bookstore managers give you free juice and treat you like a celebrity, making announcements over their loudspeaker systems so that their patrons know there is a real, live, published author in the store this very minute!

[Julie] Most aspiring authors don't realize that most signings are just plain humbling. People imagine it to all be glamour and long lines of grinning faces asking you to sign stacks of books. It is best to remember that Glamour *is a magazine, not an occupation. There are times when no one stops at your table or cares in any way that you have written a book.*

That doesn't mean the signing is a waste. It's a great time to get to know the store employees. Become friends with them; laugh with them; help them with duties to make their shift more pleasant. Even if they never read your book, they will be more likely to recommend it to their customers simply because they like you.

At one signing I had, the manager expected that I would bring my own table, which was never mentioned to me by anyone, so I arrived empty handed. He treated me like I had been caught shoplifting instead of coming to help bring business to his store. He set me up in a corner where there was no hope of me interacting with the customers, and grimaced and snarled every time he looked in my direction. It was so wholly unlike any other experience I have ever had that the two hours became the most uncomfortable of my entire life.

In situations such as this (may they be few!) it is best to stay cool-headed and well-mannered. Store managers and employees are the front-line sales people of your book. If they think ill of you, they will be unlikely to recommend you to any prospective readers. In most situations the stores will be glad you are there and will treat you like an honored guest for giving them your time. On the up side, most managers and employees have been delightful to me. I have been given very nice gifts and provided with lunch just for smiling and saying, "Hi, I'm here to sign books."

[Josi] I have a real abhorrence for book signings. I've had lousy experience after lousy experience, and even when they go well, it's awkward and uncomfortable to stand there and sell. However, my publisher requests that I promote my books, and I want to do whatever I can. If book signings help—and I believe they do—then it's worth the awkwardness and discomfort.

[Shirley] As for Oprah, well, your phone is likely to grow cobwebs while you wait. You can do things yourself on a local level to get the word out. Go out and do book signings. Offer to speak, volunteer to read at a hospital or school. Someday, Oprah might pass through your town and stop by your house to buy an autographed book from you.

Hey, you got a book published. It could happen!

[Josi] In conclusion, make sure that you're in touch with your reasons for writing. If you're writing for the money or the fame, keep sending in those sweepstakes entries, because that's not what writing is about. Even if you make millions, the time and talent you invest is far more valuable, and your book will never mean as much to anyone else as it does to you.

Those of us who have contributed to this book write because we love to write, and we love to share what we've written. Keeping this focus allows us to be really excited when we get a measly $50 royalty check in the mail or when someone finally recognizes us at the grocery store.

Write for the love of it, the joy of it, and the legacy you leave. If you do that, you'll always come out on top.

conclusion

by Gordon Ryan

Wasn't that fun?

They're not all alike, are they?—these authors who write romance, action, fantasy, historical fiction, doctrinal essays, and biographies. But they all write for a reason, and only part of it is to satisfy their own need to create. By and large the biggest part of their work is done for *you*—to entertain, to encourage, to improve your life.

But we would be remiss if we didn't add a caveat—a word of caution.

Most of us watched (and some cringed) as the American Idol auditions were held in front of a world-wide television audience. Thousands upon thousands of would-be singers stood in front of the three judges (and ultimately millions of viewers) and sang their hearts out—or at least tried to.

I'm not trying to discourage you, but in closing I think it only appropriate to be certain that you understand how much commitment is required to publish a book. Are you willing to contribute the effort, the sacrifice, the dedication? Stories about your family history, your dog's antics, or great-great-grandmother's trek across the plains may thrill your fellow office workers and your family—and of course your mother absolutely loves them. But such stories have limited interest beyond your immediate circle of family and friends. Coming up with a compelling plot line, *and stretching it into 250-400 pages*, is not as easy as one might think. It requires the total dedication that the authors in this book have been describing.

As has been pointed out in this book, rejection is perhaps the most difficult and painful part of the writing business. *Every single author represented in this book has been rejected.* Every one! If you can handle that aspect of this sometimes crusty business, then, by all means, go for it.

But—and this is the reason we prepared this book—*every single author in this book has been published.* Every one!

You can, too. That's why we have compiled our knowledge and experience—to help you get published.

So write on!

We wish you the very best in your new endeavor. We'll be rooting for you and looking for your first book. We hope it sells thousands and earns you the #2 spot on the bestseller list—right behind *ours*!

linda paulson adams

Linda was born in Baltimore, Maryland, and moved to California in 1978 at the age of nine. She attended Brigham Young University from 1986 to 1990, where she received an AA in English. (Hmmm, add that up.) She married Steve Adams in 1988 in the Manti Temple. Both lifetime active members of the Church, they have six children ages thirteen and under, two cats, two dogs, a hamster, a gerbil, and a fish living in their home in Jackson County, Missouri.

Linda has loved storytelling since childhood, loves to diagram sentences and pick grammar apart, and can spell without the aid of a spell-checker. Two difficult pregnancies in the last three years slowed her writing down a bit, but the children always come first. Her first novel, *Prodigal Journey*, was released in 2000 by Cornerstone Publishing, winning their Fiction Book of the Year Award. She finished the sequel, *Refining Fire*, in 2001. Cornerstone went out of business before its printing, and the book is now forthcoming with LDStorymakers, Inc. She has published shorter works in literary magazines such as *Irreantum*, *Meridian Magazine*, and *Lynx Eye*.

Other hobbies include reading paperbacks in a hot bubble bath, knitting, drawing, singing, and playing piano. Last year she discovered the joys of both yoga and thread crochet. She can't ballroom dance or follow an aerobic workout video to save her life. In fact she has even been known to mess up "Book of Mormon Stories" hand signs in front of live Primary children. She also can't do crafts or scrapbook or decorate her house worth beans. She adds all this because she is sometimes asked if there's anything she can't do. Plenty. But at least she can turn out a decent sentence.

Visit her website at: www.alyssastory.com

shirley bahlmann

Apart from challenging her little sisters to chalkboard drawing contests and playing Secret Agent with her little brother in Haddon Heights, New Jersey, Shirley's favorite childhood pastime was hiding in the closet to read books. When she was ten years old, she aspired to write a novel, and had the satisfaction of scrawling "The End" after 25 hand-written pages.

Shirley worked as editor of her elementary school and college newspapers and kept stacks of journals over the years. Now she is the published author of the true pioneer *Odds* series and several other books in various phases of completion. Shirley delights in the unexpected, such as the amusing comment her friend made, "You were Miss Snow College? You sure don't act like it!"

Shirley plans to keep writing for as long as her life lasts . . . and beyond, if she has anything to say about it! (After rendering a saxophone medley of Primary songs for her in-laws' missionary farewell, she also hopes she can trade in her harp for a tenor sax!)

Married to Bob Bahlmann since 1978 and the mother of six sons, Andy, Jeff, Scott, Zackary, Brian, and Michael. Shirley contemplated writing a book titled *How to Raise Boys* until she realized that she still doesn't know how.

Visit her website at: www.shirleybahlmann.com

anne bradshaw

Anne's storymaking began during her eighth year with the discovery that the younger siblings stopped squabbling when she created wild tooth-fairy tales about witches who lived in people's teeth.

For more than fifteen years Anne has written both fiction and non-fiction for the *New Era*. After taking a writing correspondence course, reading everything she could find related to the subject, and experimenting with small articles aimed at local publications, Anne decided to interview her weekly Seminary class. This became the first of many British stories appearing in the *New Era*.

"Church magazine staff are outstanding to work with," Anne says. "They taught me how to take my own pictures, and if stories weren't right, instead of rejecting them, they let me know weak areas, giving me an opportunity to fix things." Anne traveled throughout the British Isles interviewing LDS youth. "An inspiring experience," she adds. "I met some of the finest young people in the world."

Anne and her husband, Bob, moved from England to Utah in 1997 to join their four children. It was around this time that she decided to fulfill a long-nurtured desire to write a novel. Her first book, *Terracotta Summer,* set in 1960s Britain, is a fast-paced story about the O'Sheas—a family tale of trial and intrigue with a splash of romance. The sequel, *Chamomile Winter*, followed in 2002.

Anne writes articles for numerous LDS websites and is also working on a new novel and a book of short stories for LDS youth. She is grateful for a full life. Family, Church callings, writing, reading, walking, and gardening take up every minute.

Visit her website at: www.annebradshaw.com

thom duncan

Thom is one of the few mortals walking the earth who has received a writing award at least once in every decade he has been writing, since somewhere in the early 60s. Most of his writing has been in the theater, where he has enjoyed the production of over thirty of his plays at Brigham Young University, Utah Valley State College, several locations in California, and independent theaters in Utah County.

Thom is the founder of the Nauvoo Theatrical Society—a theatre company dedicated to the production of LDS-oriented plays. In 1990, his first novel was published, *Moroni Smith: In the Land of Zarahemla*, which he is currently adapting to the screen.

Thom is the father of five children and grandfather of another five—none of whom think he is as good a writer as he thinks he is.

josi kilpack

Josi's love of writing came from her love of reading—a trait passed on from her mother, and something she will always be grateful for. As a child she was too busy annoying her two older sisters or teasing her six younger siblings to pay much attention to reading (or cleaning or hair combing or finding her shoes), but from her teenage years on, Josi always seemed to have a book at her side. She always liked English in school, but it wasn't until she was married with two kids that she tried writing an actual book. Life has become a whole new experience since then.

Despite a horrible penchant for slang and lousy spelling, she has refined and tuned her craft over the years. She is currently the proud—if somewhat frazzled—mother of four children and lives in Willard, Utah.

To date Josi has published three LDS women's novels with Cedar Fort, Inc.: *Earning Eternity, Surrounded By Strangers,* and *Tempest Tossed.* She has also tried her hand at writing short stories, articles, and production pieces, for which she has received awards.

Josi and her husband, Lee, run two assisted-living facilities in Northern Utah. For non-writing fun, Josi enjoys scrapbooking, home décor, baking, and traveling.

Visit her website at: www.josiskilpack.com

rachel ann nunes

Rachel learned to read when she was four, beginning a lifetime fascination with the written word. She avidly began devouring books, and still reads everything she can lay her hands on, from children's stories to nonfiction articles on science. She began writing in the seventh grade, and is now the author of 18 published books, including the popular *Ariana* series and the picture book *Daughter of a King*, voted Best Children's Book of the Year in 2003 by the Association of Independent LDS Booksellers.

While Rachel mainly focuses on writing contemporary women's fiction with strong plots and characters, her works also include more generally focused novels such as *A Greater Love* and *A Heartbeat Away*. She also enjoys writing fantasy novels and the occasional science fiction story, which she plans to get around to publishing any day now. (Maybe after the laundry is done!)

While serving an LDS mission to Portugal, Rachel met her husband, TJ. They now live in Utah Valley and are the parents of six awesome children—three boys and three girls. She loves camping with her family, traveling, and meeting new people, and, of course, writing. "If the gospel is like breathing," she says, "writing is like eating. To live I must write." Rachel writes Monday through Friday in a home office, often with a child on her lap, taking frequent breaks to build Lego towers, practice phonics, or jump on the trampoline. She believes that raising her family is the most important thing she will ever do.

Her 19th book, the debut of a new LDS series, will be released in the near future.

For more information, or to join her e-mailing list, visit: www.rachelannnunes.com

lisa j. peck

As a child, Lisa's rapt interest in storytelling hindered her ability to learn to read. She loved to make up stories to the *See Jane Run* books, rather than read the boring text as it was written. She thought her own reason why the girl was so sad on the swing was much more entertaining, although her mother didn't agree. She finally did learn how to read, and eventually earned an English degree at Brigham Young University.

She has been published in numerous magazines and won many awards. She is the Executive Producer of the best-selling film *Christmas Mission* and the Heartland Award Winner Film *Cowboys and Angels.* She also wrote the film *Only Once*. She is the author of *The Truth Seeker Trilogy: Dangerous Memories, More Precious than Diamonds,* and *Nauvoo's Magic,* published by Cedar Fort, Inc. Her book *Lucy Mack Smith* in the *Mothers of the Prophets* series will soon be released, also from Cedar Fort. She has also published *Life with the Kids* and *Lovin' for a Lifetime* with Horizon, and the picture book *What about Me?* with Bristone Films. She published *A Challenge for Brittany,* book two in the *Choose the Right* series, with Bookcraft. Other works can be found in *Sunshine For the Latter-Day Saint Child's Soul* with Deseret Book.

Recently remarried, she is raising her six beautiful children in Utah with her husband. She also runs a content critiquing service where she helps new authors bring their work up to publishing quality.

Contact her at: pup7777@aol.com

tristi pinkston

Tristi has been writing since the age of five, when she wrote and illustrated the compelling saga, *Sue the Dog.* She spent most of her childhood and youth with her nose in one book after another, hardly ever coming to earth for any practical purpose whatsoever, and most certainly not ever to clean her room. One of the best Christmas presents she ever got was a robin's egg blue manual typewriter the year she was ten.

Her first published book, *Nothing to Regret,* was released in 2002. Her second book, *Strength to Endure,* will go to press around the end of 2004, and she plans to publish many more.

Tristi lives with her three very active children and her very active husband in Pleasant Grove, where she is a stay-at-home mom with her fingers constantly busy with typing, rubber stamping, cooking, cleaning, and sometimes just twitching out of built-up creative energy. She's even been known to type in her sleep, hitting her fingers against her pillow (not loudly). Her biggest career goal is to live long enough to write all the stories she has floating in her head. (Good luck with that!)

Visit her website at: www.tristipinkston.com

bj rowley

When it comes to the writing world, BJ is a fortunate late bloomer, having never written anything of real consequence before his black-balloon 40th birthday. In fact, looking waaaaay back to his high school days (when dinosaurs roamed the earth), he distinctly remembers how much he disliked his creative writing class. But BJ has been an avid reader from the get-go, devouring adventure books and spy novels as he traveled around the country and the world (business related, not jet-setting).

One day BJ was thinking about a book he'd recently finished, and thought, "You know, I think I could write as well as any of these guys," (we're talking Clive Cussler and Tom Clancy here!) "but what on earth would I write about?"

A few days later at suppertime, BJ announced to his family, "I'm going to write a book." That was followed by silence, incredulous stares, and forks stopped in midair, after which one son laughed and said, "Yeah, right, Dad. Whatever."

Undaunted, he forged ahead. And the inspiration came. He has since released five adventure novels targeted at teens and young adults, including *Sixteen In No Time*, *STING!* and the popular three-volume *Light Traveler Adventure Series.*

BJ also edited and ghost-published the novelization of the movie *God's Army*, by Geoffrey Card, in cooperation with Excel Entertainment Publishing and Zion Films.

BJ also enjoys photography, aviation, playing various musical instruments, composing music, watching movies and home videos, playing board games, spending time with his family, and baby-sitting his grandson . . . oh, and sleeping in on Saturdays.

Visit his website at: www.bjrowley.com

gordon ryan

Gordon published his first novel, *Dangerous Legacy*, in 1994. The publisher then accepted a novella, *Threads of Honor*, and signed a contract for an historical fiction series entitled *Spirit of Union. Threads of Honor* went to #1 for the publisher for six weeks in 1996. In 1997, *Spirit of Union: Destiny 1895-1898*, jumped to the top ten on their regional list. That was followed by *Spirit of Union: Conflict 1898-1919*, and *Spirit of Union: Heritage 1919-1940*. In collaboration with his daughter, Kate Armitage, he has also written *Upon the Isles of the Sea*, a Book of Mormon fiction story. His two new novels, *A Question of Consequence* and *State of Rebellion,* are due out in spring 2004. His work in progress is *Uncivil Liberties,* a story of terrorist infiltration of the United States of America.

Gordon served as City Manager in three cities, and was Chief Executive in a resort community in southern California. He also served as a member of the American Embassy staff in Dublin, Ireland. After high school, he served in the Marine Corps, and later in the U.S. Air Force during the Vietnam conflict. An accomplished public speaker, he delivered editorial comment on a network television news show in Sacramento, occasionally guest-hosted a weekly radio call-in show in Alaska, and frequently accepts invitations for public presentations.

Born in New York, Gordon holds a Bachelors degree with Honors in Political Science and has completed graduate work in Public Administration. After living in Norway, Thailand, Taiwan, Ireland, Alaska, and throughout the United States, Gordon currently resides in New Zealand, with his wife, Colleen Sterling, of Christchurch, New Zealand.

Visit his website at: www.gordonryan.com

marsha ward

Marsha first began telling stories during grade school years, when she would bake a batch of sugar cookies, take them to her friend's house, and serve up her tales to her pals with the cookies. These summer episodes, along with being the editor of the fifth-grade class newspaper, foretold her future career in journalism, as she became a writer and editor for four different LDS newspapers.

Throughout her adulthood, Marsha loved fiction and history. She studied creative writing with Stephan Overholser, William Greenleaf, Kate Horsley, and others. Marsha attended Phoenix College and Northern Arizona University and served a mission in Colombia and Venezuela, where her poetry was published in the Venezuelan periodical, *La Cosecha.* Marsha has also read her work at Yavapai College and the Sharlot Hall Museum in Prescott, Arizona.

All told, Marsha has over 900 published works in a variety of publications in the United States and has won numerous awards. After 38 years of polishing, she finally published her first novel, *The Man from Shenandoah,* in early 2003. Proving she wasn't a one-novel wonder, she published *Ride to Raton* in the fall of 2003, which has been equally well-received.

In addition to writing, Marsha works with other writers as a mentor, contest judge, and workshop presenter. In 1986, she founded the American Night Writers Association (ANWA)—a network for LDS women writers.

Marsha enjoys receiving feedback from readers, travel, playing with her above-average grandchildren, and working on her upcoming novels. She currently lives in Mesa, Arizona.

Visit her website at: www.MarshaWard.com

linda shelley whiting

Linda was born in Evanston, Illinois and grew up in Mesa, Arizona. At age eleven, she wrote a paper for school on what she wanted to be when she grew up. She already knew. The title read, "Why I Want to be a Writer."

Linda graduated from Brigham Young University in 1970 with a degree in journalism, then served a mission for the LDS Church in Colorado and New Mexico. Shortly after her mission, Linda published her first freelance historical feature, with many more to follow through the years.

In 1972, she married J. Brent Whiting. They are blessed with six children: Wendy, Valerie, Roger, Carrie, Shelley, and Beth.

Her passion is writing—particularly about Mormon history. But she is also crazy about art, family history, and growing things.

While doing research in the BYU library for a magazine article on painter Minerva Teichert, Linda had a spiritual experience concerning David W. Patten. Pondering on what happened between those library stacks that day, she came to the conclusion she was to write a biography of this great Apostle's life. The research for that book took ten years, the writing only eighteen months. The book was written for ordinary members of the Christ of Jesus Christ of Latter-day Saints and others interested in early Mormon history. Cedar Fort, Inc. published *David W. Patten, Apostle and Martyr* in May of 2003.

Linda is currently in the research phase for her next book—a history of the Mormon Settlement of the Salt River Valley, Arizona.

Visit her website at: www.davidwpatten.com

julie wright

Julie's very first memories are of reading and being read to. At the age of 15, she decided she could write a book as good as the ones she was reading, and set off to start her first novel. She cast it aside for the trivial lifestyle of a teenager (flipping burgers to afford the gas to drive absolutely nowhere in her car) and didn't pick it up again until after she was married.

Julie finished her first book *To Catch a Falling Star*, and began her second novel, *Loved Like That*, while hanging out on movie sets, working as a stand-in in *Touched By An Angel.* Her third novel is in the publication process and should be released soon. She is working on her fourth, fifth, and sixth books simultaneously.

Julie won Media Play's short fantasy fiction contest for "A Man In Mandalore" in 2000, and Cedar Fort's Popular Fiction Award in 2002. She has had several articles and poetry published, and paid for her parking tickets in college by writing poetry for the *Friend* and *New Era* magazines. She has also enjoyed presenting firesides for the Young Women's program and conducting writing workshops for schools.

Julie's goal is to write a novel a year until they pry the pen from her cold, dead fingers. She is supported in this by the love of her life and the three most intelligent, beautiful, perfect-when-sleeping children in the world—all kidding and prejudice aside.

She loves reading, writing, taking long baths, eating, hiking, dancing with her kids in the kitchen, and snuggling with her husband while watching videos. She loves to travel, and maintains that if she does not leave her time zone at least once every six months she will go insane and take everyone she knows with her. She also enjoys watching her husband make dinner.

Visit her website at: www.juliewright.com

If you would like to direct a publishing-related question to LDStorymakers, feel free to e-mail them at:

questions@ldstorymakers.com

They will be more than happy to assist you.

For more information regarding LDStorymakers, their products, and upcoming events, see their website at:

http://www.ldstorymakers.com